Friends, & Neighbors Folks Down the Road

Stories and photography by

Ed Okonowicz and Jerry Rhodes

Myst and Lace Publishers, Inc.

Friends, Neighbors and Folks Down the Road
First Edition

ISBN 1-890690-12-0

Published by
Myst and Lace Publishers, Inc.
1386 Fair Hill Lane
Elkton, MD 21921

Printed in the U. S. A.
by Thomson-Shore, Inc.

Stories and Photography
(unless noted otherwise)
by Ed Okonowicz

Design and Layout
by Kathleen Okonowicz

Cover and Section Photographs
by Kathy Flickinger Atkinson

Additional Stories
by Jerry Rhodes and Jaime Cherundolo

Dedications

For Bill Lowe and Victoria Lusardi
Thanks for the memories.

To Emma Elizabeth Kuchak Okonowicz
Welcome to the family.

Acknowledgments

A number of fascinating and talented folks provided valuable assistance throughout this project. Some suggested interesting people to interview, others supplied photographs and some of my closest friends helped with proofreading and editing.

While I took most of the book's photographs during interviews, other pictures were supplied, or taken, by those listed below. Credit is noted next to their respective pictures featured in chapters throughout the book.

Kathy Flickinger Atkinson	Kathleen Okonowicz
Jack Buxbaum	Greg Ositko
Jaime Cherundolo	Lois Podedwomy
Christopher Cook	Jerry Rhodes
Lisa McKeown Dolor	Ray Russo
Larry Foster	Ron Thomas, MAAR Associates Inc.
Ed and Joanna Howe	University of Delaware Office of Public Relations
Family members of Victoria Lusardi	Chuck Wehrle

Barbara Burgoon, John Brennan, Marianna Dyal, Sue Moncure, Kathleen Okonowicz and Ted Stegura offered proofreading and editing suggestions. Their valuable contributions are particularly appreciated.

Linda Chatfield, executive director of the Delaware Agricultural Museum and Village, hosted the July 12, 2003, photo shoot in Dover, Delaware. Pictures taken that day are on the book's cover, at the beginning page of each section and in the "Photo Album" pages at the end of the book.

The artist and designer, Kathleen Okonowicz, deserves special credit. Jerry Rhodes, Jaime Cherundolo and I supplied the raw material, but my wonderful wife took the hundreds of individual pieces and created this attractive final product. Without her, the pieces of the book would be scattered over several computers awaiting attention.

Appreciation must also be extended to the great friends, neighbors and folks down the road who agreed to be interviewed and share their experiences. The best part of the project was getting to meet all of them, learn what they do and make some new friends along the way.

Finally, two of the people interviewed during this project passed away before publication, Bill Lowe of Lewes, Delaware, and Victoria Lusardi of Newark, Delaware. Their interesting achievements and fascinating comments are captured in these pages and serve as examples of all of the wonderfully fascinating neighbors in our midst that are waiting to be discovered.

Table of Contents

Neighbors

Folks Down the Road

Introduction

Despite the horrifying headlines in the daily newspapers and the sensational and negative topics that run continuously on the 24-hour cable news networks, the world is filled with good, caring, talented and fascinating people. These everyday folks are not involved in violence or crime, and they don't race toward TV cameras and reporters like Hollywood personalities or sports superstars.

But these special, and often overlooked persons next door, have very remarkable stories to tell. A few are heroes, others are eccentrics, some are patriots, and certain ones have proved that one single person, dedicated to a cause and willing to work hard, can make a significant difference.

Occasionally, television networks will close their newscasts with short, memorable feature segments about these unique characters that march to a different drummer. And, frankly, that's the main reason they are pulled into the spotlight—because they stand out from the crowd.

People love to hear about the dog that saved its master from a fire, the grandmother who beat up a would-be robber and the man whose basement museum houses a lifelong collection of 100,000 treasured widgets or special souvenirs.

> *There's a proverb that states: 'A prophet is without honor in his own country.' In plain old, ordinary language, that means: It's easy to overlook the expert down the street.*
>
> *There is no reason to travel to far away places with strange sounding names to enjoy top notch material in the human interest category.*

With information pouring through the Internet, cable channels and satellite dish programming, on their special feature programs we can learn about intriguing people located around the globe. Unfortunately, this instantaneous access to the world's big picture increases the chances that we will not notice the fascinating folks, nifty neighbors and colorful characters that live right down the road.

Years ago, in small towns and city neighborhoods, everyone knew almost everything about the people next door or the folks down the road or those who lived a few blocks up the street. People who weren't related would watch out for each other and keep an eye on the neighborhood kids. There was a stronger sense of community.

Over the years, with the arrival of a mobile society, settlements in the suburbs and improvements in transportation, this sense of togetherness, of community, has been lost. It's become a victim of the combination of progress and changing lifestyles.

Today people tend to keep to themselves. Some because they want to and others because they have to. It seems that almost every free moment is occupied by convenient distractions or responsibilities—from hobbies and computer games to delivering children to dance lessons and soccer practice and, in many cases, having to work more than one job.

There are fewer opportunities to socialize and pass the time talking "like they did in the old days" on the front porch swing with "the neighbors."

Times change, people adapt and time-consuming customs eventually disappear. But certain things stay the same—in particular, the tendency to overlook what is right in front of one's eyes.

There's a proverb that states, "A prophet is without honor in his own country." In plain old, ordinary language, that means: It's easy to overlook the expert down the street.

It's human nature to take for granted what's worthwhile around the bend and not pay much attention to the accomplishments or really neat stuff being done by members of our very own family.

But "locals," or "that guy down the road," as they are called, can match up with the best that sophisticated TV producers have to offer. There is no reason to travel to far away places with strange sounding names to enjoy top notch material in the human interest category.

Many of these folks live down the block, around the bend or, at most, within the driving time required for a quick weekend daytrip. But I suggest you head off and find them before it's too late, because our interesting characters are under ever-increasing pressure. You see,

· sterile malls are devouring small businesses that possess their own special characters,

· creeping enforcement of political correctness is causing bland dialog to obliterate our colorful language and limit spontaneous truthful outburts,

· fast food chains are gobbling up regional cuisine,

· high technology is delivering toys and gizmos

that foster isolation through individualized—rather than group and family—entertainment and

· work demands and economic pressures are exterminating shared family time.

Soon, only old movies or a time machine will allow us to escape this ever-changing, fast-paced world. There will be no hamlets left where we can step back, for only a few hours, into the past to talk with people who care for the simpler, better days gone by.

Despite the grim present day environment, some of the people in this book were smart enough to never leave the best of times. They have stuck with the tried and true. Several have carved out niches for themselves that are protected from the cold, impersonal intrusions of modern life. And many others have claimed title to being an expert about something that no one else seems to care about.

In these pages, you will meet people who march to a different drummer. Some, in fact, seem to perform in their very own one-man band.

Each is unique, special and one of a kind.

You will not find anyone representing those modern, urbanized, high-tech gathering places and work sites where sterile conformity, an aloof attitude and stylish clothing are badges of being cool, hip and in.

In *Friends, Neighbors and Folks Down the Road*, what people in the know say is "in" is definitely "out."

In these stories, dialects have been preserved, old-time traditions and individual excellence have been recognized and those overlooked have claimed a few pages of space in the spotlight.

> *In these pages, you will meet people who march to a different drummer. Some, in fact, seem to perform in their very own one-man band. Each is unique, special and one of a kind.*

During the writing of *Disappearing Delmarva: Portraits of the Peninsula People* in 1997, my goal was to capture the region's threatened occupations, customs and small town/family businesses before they passed on. During that search, I came across other interesting folks who didn't quite fit the endangered cultural category, but their stories certainly are worth sharing with others.

In this follow-up volume, I once again played connect-the-dots with human beings. Each person I interviewed suggested another person or two to include in this book. As a result of those recommendations, you will meet some of the most fascinating people I have had the good fortune to encounter.

A few are driven by personal zeal to preserve a family or cultural tradition, some have turned an idea into a reality and others calmly pass their days doing what comes naturally, without a care about what others think or say. Mostly, these are average, everyday Joes and Janes, except that they are constantly in motion, exhibiting plenty of spark and spunk and a never-ending list of new projects to pursue.

Every village, town and city has its special characters, heroes, eccentrics and notables. In major urban centers, they are more numerous and compete for attention. In smaller towns, they're more noticeable and better known.

Here are stories of my neighbors—your neighbors, too—who live in the mid-Atlantic region. Most of their acquaintances and colleagues and next door neighbors have no idea of the significant achievements some of these folks have accomplished.

I found them all within a two-hour car ride from my driveway. And if you head on down the road with serious people-watching in mind, you can catch up with them—and many others like them—along the way.

If you pause at a red light and scan the shoulder of the road, you'll notice the man behind the card table selling his handcarved replicas of fishing boats.

If you listen carefully to what others say, and not focus on how you will respond, you'll find out about the war hero who lives two doors down the street.

If you pass by the fast food chain outlet and take a little extra time to smell the aroma at a family owned restaurant, you'll discover that champion, county fair pie maker around the next bend in the road.

If you want to know what makes a person enjoy something no one else seems to think too much about, you'll enjoy *Friends, Neighbors and Folks Down the Road*.

And if your interest is sparked, you just might take the time to get to know your neighbors, or the folks up the road, and discover a fascinating story or two in the process.

If you do, happy hunting. It's lots of fun—and the rewards are closer and greater than you can imagine.

—Ed Okonowicz,
Fair Hill, Maryland,
at the northern edge
of the Delmarva Peninsula
Fall 2003

Author's note: This book was started in 1998 and delayed several times. I want to thank Jerry Rhodes, my good friend who coauthored our biography *Matt Zabitka: SPORTS, 60 Years of Headlines and Deadlines.* Without Jerry's fine writing, this book would still be "in the works."

Also, Jaime Cherundolo, a University of Delaware graduate, allowed us to use her feature writing class article about Mrs. Victoria Lusardi, the first Miss Delaware beauty queen. Jaime's excellent work is featured as a chapter in this book.

Friends

Photograph by Kathy F. Atkinson

George Reynolds

Elk Mills, Maryland

UFOs, Arrowheads and More

It was in the fall of 1988 that I first met George M. Reynolds Sr., now 80, at his old farmhouse in Elk Mills, Maryland. The village is not far from the portion of the Mason-Dixon Line that runs north to south separating Delaware and Maryland.

The topic of our first meeting was "ghosts." I was doing a story for the Wilmington *News Journal* and I was told that George had a few spirited residents in his home.

We hit it off immediately, since I, too, am a believer in the bizarre, unusual and unexplained. Over the years, we've become good friends. When we have a family event, George is a welcome addition. When my wife, Kathleen, and I were married in 1991, George, a licensed minister, performed our wedding ceremony. And, whenever I am in need of a lead for an unusual chapter in one of my other ghost/folklore books, George always seems to come through with an excellent suggestion.

While interviewing George during the summer of 1998 for this book, he jokingly said, "I guess I would fall under the section, the most interesting person you've ever met!"

George had hit the bull's-eye.

How do you accurately describe a man who, in the January 1976 issue of *The Upper Shoreman*, was featured in an article with the headline: "George Reynolds—Man of Activities."

The writer, Gladys Anderson said, "Perhaps the best single word describing George Reynolds is 'active' and that even falls short of doing him justice."

In the intervening years, while most people have slowed down, George has moved his level of activity to a higher plane and one that people half his age would have difficulty matching.

To list his awards and publications would take up more space than I've allotted, but worth noting is his role as one of the founders and a past president of the Archeological Society of Maryland. He has served in various administrative, research or public speaking roles with the Elk Creek Preservation Society, Historical Society of Cecil County and Northeastern Chapter of the Archeological Society of Maryland. He also is founder and director of the Mutual UFO Network (MUFON) Northeast Maryland Chapter.

George's home is shared with numerous decoys that he's carved, electronic equipment for his short-wave (W3WYA) communication activities, thousands of American Indian arrowheads and artifacts that he has personally discovered and books on subjects ranging from art and history to electronics and unexplained phenomena. In an attractive flower bed in his front yard are numerous petroglyphs—large gray rocks with Indian markings—that he retrieved from the nearby Susquehanna River.

In *At the Head of the Bay*, the 1996 book on Cecil County, Maryland, history, George's eight photographs of his artifacts are featured in the first chapter representing, he explained, "seven periods of prehistoric man over the last 11,000 years in the mid-Atlantic region."

A World War II Navy veteran, he received much of his education in the service, since he was forced to drop out of high school and work on Cecil County farms.

"I loved to learn," George said. "I read a lot, taught myself and asked a lot of questions." After

coming home from the Navy, he earned his high school equivalency certificate and eventually took college courses at the universities of Delaware, Michigan and Arizona and at the Massachusetts Institute of Technology.

In 1972, he retired from his job as an electronics development technician at the U. S. Army Ballistics Research Laboratory at Aberdeen Proving Ground.

Not one to sit idle, George completed a four-year course of study in theology and, in 1973, became a licensed minister, fulfilling a promise he made to the Lord while on sub duty in World War II.

While county residents today know of George's work with MUFON and ghosts and history, few realize that before Interstate 95 was built, George mobilized a citizen's group to survey the area for American Indian villages.

"They were going to cut a path across the county that was to be 300 feet wide and 17 miles long, crossing five major rivers and creeks, and no archaeology was going to be done," George recalled.

Taking the initiative, he raised $500, got matching funds from the state and convinced a number of volunteers to "walk every inch of the highway area."

While they didn't find any evidence of villages, they found several artifacts and two quarry sites where the Indians had come to the area to secure jasper and quartz. George described the Eastern Shore and Delmarva as a "melting pot of culture," and he testified before state committees in Annapolis about his discoveries and the importance of archaeology.

"Whenever a quantity of earth is moved," George said, "when they build roads or new homes or any type of construction, there is often a record of the past in the form of artifacts. If a careful study is made, you can learn what was there before. Holding in your hand something from an earlier age serves as a link to other eras. Understanding archaeology also brings you closer to nature, and that also is important."

George said he is proud that he had a role in getting the state of Maryland to recognize the need for a state archaeologist. He recalled speaking to officials in Annapolis on the subject. "I told them," George said, " 'You people think you're so advanced and sophisticated. In West Virginia, where you think they're nothing but backwoods hillbillies, they've got two state archaeologists and a state museum. Here in Maryland we don't have an archaeologist or museum!' "

Laughing at the memory, he added, "That got their attention."

His interest in Unidentified Flying Objects began in physics classes before he was forced to quit high school.

"I used to look at the stars and they would amaze me," he said. "When I was in Okinawa in 1945, I was on the *USS Beaver*, a sub tender. It was hot in the engine room, so I went topside and laid down on the deck. I looked up at the stars, 14,000 miles from home and focused on the

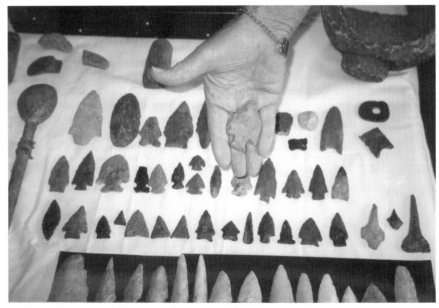

A display of arrowheads from George's extensive collection

brightest star. I noticed the moves it was making, not just a straight line, but sharp turns to the left and right. I'll never forget that.

"I went into Hiroshima, where they dropped the Atom Bomb, riding on a Japanese truck. The ground was too radioactive to walk on. I wondered if someone from another world might have been attracted to us from the size of the explosion and came down to see what in the world we were doing."

A few years later, there were sightings of flying discs over Washington, D. C. As part of his work in the research lab at Aberdeen Proving Ground, George would talk with scientists and discuss the subject of UFOs. In 1953, he joined the Aerial Phenomenon Research Organization and became a field investigator.

To those learned sophisticates who scoff at people who believe in or study reports of UFOs, George often quotes a famous scientist. "Einstein said, 'To investigate the unknown is the true love and joy of science.'"

During the last four-and-a-half decades, he has investigated hundreds of reports by people who live throughout the East Coast. He has visited sites in Pennsylvania, New England, Virginia and Florida, speaking to those who claim they have seen UFOs and others who state that they have been abducted.

At UFO conferences throughout the country, George is on a first-name basis with the leading researchers and authors in the UFO field. Former NASA employees, retired military officers, college professors and authors speak to George as a colleague and equal.

A few years ago, he hosted a day-long UFO conference in North East, Maryland, and he turned attendees away at the door. Each month, he holds a meeting for guests and members of his Northeast Maryland MUFON chapter. And, more recently, as a MUFON field investigator, he has conducted interviews on UFO sightings and crop circle activity in Cecil and Harford counties in Maryland and in New Castle County, Delaware.

"Something is happening," George said. "The government may be trying to protect us. But, eventually, it will all come out. It's happening to too many people. Initially, when you say you're involved with UFO research, some people think you're some kind of a nut. But I believe that there is more out there than just us, and truly educated people will keep an open mind.

"To me it's a challenge. Are there other planets, other worlds, other dimensions? To some degree, youngsters may be the key. Their brains aren't contaminated yet."

Having done so much, some find it amazing that George continually talks about his new project, his upcoming speech, his next monthly meeting, his scheduled newsletter.

"I need to write all this up, about the Indian artifacts, about how we know something is 6,000 years old—to put the things I know into the proper context before I pass on to the Happy Hunting Grounds. I guess if I had the time, I'd like to be able to write everything down that I've learned, and pass it along. But that takes time, and my problem is I have to regulate my time. Other people are always pulling my chain. I've got to go wide open all day, all the time.

"But, if I could, I think I'd like to leave behind the information on the archaeology. And, if there's time, I'd like to write a story, or even a book, on the history of Cecil County. I know so much that I collected, I'd like to include things that have been totally forgotten."

And when he's in the Happy Hunting Grounds, what does George hope folks will say?

"When I'm gone, I'd like people to say, 'George Reynolds, he was a nice old fella—ornery as hell, and he talked a lot, but he was a good guy.'"

Elbert Chance at the microphone with spotter Bob Siemen in the Delaware Stadium press box

Elbert Chance

Newark, Delaware

'Voice of Delaware Stadium'

For a half century, he saw practically every Delaware Stadium touchdown and fumble and he announced the score of nearly every home field victory and defeat. To many Blue Hen football fans, his familiar voice and trademark announcement: "GOOD AFTERNOON, LADIES AND GENTLEMEN. WELCOME TO DELAWARE STADIUM, HOME OF THE FIGHTIN' BLUE HENS!" marked the official start of college football in Newark.

But at the end of the 2002 season, a UD football tradition ended when Elbert Chance, longtime Delaware Stadium announcer, passed the microphone on to a successor after 50 years in the press box.

Since 1953, the first full year the UD team played all its home games in the facility, hundreds of thousands of Blue and Gold fans were greeted by Elbert, 76, who is still known as the "Voice of the Fightin' Blue Hens" and the "Voice of Delaware Stadium."

The former alumni director, who retired from that position in 1985, said he honestly couldn't recall the exact circumstances that placed him in the stadium announcer's chair. In some way, he said, it was related to his dual role as sports information director and assistant director of public relations, his first job when he joined the UD staff in 1952.

"I used to joke that I was the lowest paid university employee with two offices," Elbert said, smiling. A trim man with a full head of swept-back graying hair, he seemed a bit surprised at the number of games he's announced.

With playoffs and an average of six home field contests per season, Elbert estimates he covered more than 300 games through 2002. That's more home

football games than retired long-time, head coach Tubby Raymond directed in Delaware Stadium.

"I missed three games since it all began. Once when I was sick with the flu or something," he recalled. "One time, I took my daughter, Susan, to college at Ohio University for her freshman year, and the third one was to sing with the Brandywiners at a memorial service for Chick Laird, who was a longtime friend and a major contributor to the university."

Listening to Elbert talk enthusiastically about Delaware football is both entertaining and amazing. Since he's called so many plays, he's able to describe game-turning events and upsets with such fine detail that the listener thinks the action occurred only hours before.

When asked to share a favorite memory from his five-decade career, Elbert smiled, then said, "I even announced one game away."

That occurred at Muhlenberg College, when he went with friends to watch the Blue Hens in action on the road.

"A few minutes before the game," he said, "there was an announcement, 'Would Mr. Chance please report to the press box!'"

He learned the regular announcer was absent and, since they knew he worked the games at Delaware, the host college asked him to substitute. Elbert said he was hesitant, not knowing the other team members and concerned that he might sound partial toward the Blue Hens.

"I told them their fans would not be happy with me," Elbert recalled, "but they said they'd give me a spotter to help me identify the Muhlenberg kids. The other thing was, I was expecting Delaware to just

beat their brains out, because we had a very good team and were the favorite in the game. And it turned out that they upset us 14 to 13." He paused to laugh at the memory. Then, shaking his head, he added, "And I had to call that game."

Elbert's football Saturday routine would begin about 90 minutes before kickoff when he made the long climb to the press box. The 110 concrete steps ascend past rows marked A to Z and then AA-PP.

"When I went up at the start of the day," he said, "I usually stopped half-way up, turned around and checked the condition of the field. That also gave me a chance to catch my breath. The toughest grind was the last part of the climb, up the steps into the press box. There's nobody who goes up there that's not puffing. It's a pretty good hike."

Once inside, he talked to the newspaper and radio people, reviewed the day's scheduled events, went over pregame announcements and checked the team rosters with his long-time spotter Bob Siemen.

Conversations with the visiting sports information director insured the correct pronunciation of the names of the opposing players.

About 20 minutes before kickoff, Elbert switched on the microphone and broadcasted his trademark welcome, marking the official beginning of game day in Newark.

Elbert acknowledged he's often been asked why he spent a good portion of many fall Saturdays, seated in a crammed press box, calling out names and numbers when he could be enjoying the contest like thousands of other carefree fans.

"It's been fun," he replied, without hesitation. "It's nice to see the success of the team, and I've had football players, who I've met later, tell me, 'When we hear your voice, we get all cranked up and ready to play.'

"My philosophy on announcing at our stadium is that this is not professional football. I don't try to be absolutely formal, and just announce first down, sec-

Elbert Chance in Delaware Stadium

Photograph by Kathy F. Atkinson, University of Delaware

ond down. I try to give the people information and color.

"I've also had to make a couple of announcements that were really funny. One time it was reported to us that they had found a pocketbook, and if people would call security they would turn it over to the owner. So I said, 'Ladies and gentlemen, your attention please. We have found a black, strapless . . . .' And everybody goes, 'Ooooh!' and I said, ' . . . pocketbook!' And there was a groan from the crowd."

On another occasion, Elbert recalled when the Hens were winning a game and it was obvious late in the fourth quarter that there was going to be a playoff game the following week in the stadium.

"We were always careful when making announcements about upcoming games," Elbert said, "because we didn't want to rub salt in the wounds of the opponents, nor did we want to stir them to greater effort. Dave Nelson [late athletic director] said that with four minutes remaining I could announce that the playoff game would be here next week and that those who have season parking tickets will be able to park for $2. So I made the announcement, and everybody booed. I guess they wanted the parking for nothing.

"And Dave turns around to me and says, 'Tell 'em if they don't stop booing, I'm gonna raise it to THREE!' "

"So I said, 'Let me take care of this.' So I calculated the price and I said, 'Ladies and gentlemen, let us reason together about season parking. During the course of the year, your parking has cost you $2. 67

for every home game. At next week's game you get a 67- cent bargain.'

"They all cheered, and Dave shook his head and grinned. Later, a fellow told me he had never heard, in any stadium, someone over the loudspeaker say, 'Let us reason together.' "

'I guess I'm a throwback to the old alumni who really felt loyal to the university. I feel if I can make any contribution to that kind of spirit, it's worthwhile. I dealt with some of the old Delaware College grads in my early years in the alumni office. They were loyal in ways that I think some of today's students wouldn't understand. They had that Blue and Gold blood running in their veins, and I hope, in a way, I'm helping to carry that on.'

—Elbert Chance

Smiling as he shared the memories, Elbert said his enthusiasm for his weekend avocation has never waned.

"I looked forward to it. I've had some of the players tell me my announcements encouraged them and recognized what they had done, that they appreciated that. I figured if I can contribute to the success of the program without being so partial that it's obvious in the announcements, then it's helpful. I became better about that than I used to be. In the beginning, I probably showed my Blue and Gold colors. I know I irritated the sports information director from Rutgers, who was as fanatic about the Scarlet Knights as I am about the Blue Hens. I couldn't eliminate a little edge from my announcements when we trounced 'em."

If someone is looking for the one of the best seats in the house, especially during colder weather, the Bob Kelley Memorial Press Box—named after the late, well- known radio announcer—is the place.

"The view is good," Elbert said. "We're seated just off the 50, and I can see everything. We see more than the head coach does. Of course I had a spotter. Bob Siemen was my spotter for more than 10 years."

Because of a larger number of commercials in recent years, Elbert said the announcer's job became

more complicated. There also was the need to announce individual and team records, plus publicity requested by the cheerleaders, band and student and alumni organizations.

Each summer, soon after the Fourth of July, Elbert said he would turn his attention toward the coming season. During the spring of his last year, a planning meeting with UD's Athletic Director Edgar Johnson led to a discussion about Elbert's future.

"Edgar and I talked about the future seasons," Elbert said. "He asked, 'Do you know anyone who has done this for 50 years? That's a long time.' He didn't ask me to leave. My wife said I should go out while I'm on my game. It's been 50 seasons and that's a good record. I've enjoyed it. But I didn't leave for any specific reason, it was a number of factors that sort of came together at the same time.

> *'It is Elbert's presence at Delaware Stadium as announcer on game day that defines him. That splendid voice has become a signature of Delaware Stadium. As season ticket holders, my family and I have enjoyed the sound and comfort of his words. From opening ceremonies, to play-by-play, to commentaries, he has been part of creating a unique atmosphere uniting players and fans, students, staff and faculty, alumni and friends for an enjoyable experience.'*
>
> *—Bernie Dworsky*
> *Newark Touchdown Club*

"Most people asked me how long I had been doing it," he said, then smiled and added, "I always told them I'd like to last as long as Tubby. Things seemed to come together last year. Plus, my wife was pleased with my decision."

"He has loved every minute of it and I think it's been 50 glorious years," Prue Chance said. "I think he does a good job, but he loves it so. Anything you love you do well. I think he would have enjoyed continuing, and I told him he should go out on a high. Everything changes, and we have to adapt to change. I also think it was time for him to relax and enjoy the game without having to worry about the

announcements. And I wanted to sit in the audience with him."

Newark resident Bernie Dworsky is a former president of the Newark Touchdown Club and a long-time UD football fan. He described Elbert as "the official historian and storyteller of University of Delaware athletic exploits in the Touchdown Club."

"But," Dworsky added, "it is Elbert's presence at Delaware Stadium as announcer on game day that defines him. That splendid voice has become a signature of Delaware Stadium. As season ticket holders, my family and I have enjoyed the sound and comfort of his words. From opening ceremonies, to play-by-play, to commentaries, he has been part of creating a unique atmosphere uniting players and fans, students, staff and faculty, alumni and friends for an enjoyable experience."

Scott Selheimer, UD sports information director, echoed the comments of many fans who found Elbert's presence a very important ingredient of Delaware Stadium's appeal.

"So much of what makes college football so great is the atmosphere," Selheimer explained. "The things you see in and around the stadium, the sounds you hear, the smell of the air. Elbert was that sound you heard, the familiar voice that made it official, you were at Delaware Stadium watching the Blue Hens play football. I've heard many alumni say that when they come into the stadium, sometimes after many years away, and heard Elbert's voice, they knew they

were back home. Elbert has meant so much to the University, not only in his role as public address announcer, but with his work with the alumni office, with athletics, and his superb writing. "

Elbert downplayed the importance of his role, adding that he was just a volunteer who enjoyed his part-time job.

"I guess I'm a throwback to the old alumni who really felt loyal to the university," he said. "I feel if I can make any contribution to that kind of spirit, it's worthwhile. I dealt with some of the old Delaware College grads in my early years in the alumni office. They were loyal in ways that I think some of today's students wouldn't understand. They had that Blue and Gold blood running in their veins, and I hope, in a way, I'm helping to carry that on. "

But football is only one of Elbert's interests. An avid golfer and sought after singer, he also is a prolific writer, having written books and contributed articles and columns to the Wilmington *News Journal* and *Newark Post*. In 2002, he completed a definitive book on the history of Fightin' Blue Hen football. The hardbound volume, *One Hundred Plus: The Story of Delaware Football*, contains more than 120 photographs and accounts of 35 captivating games plus updated statistics, anecdotes and a fair share of analysis.

When asked if he would miss his familiar weekend role, Chance said, without pausing, "I won't know until I'm not there. But it will enable me to relax a little bit more on Saturday. I enjoy watching basketball games, and I'm not announcing there. "

Has he ever made an error during a game?

Rolling his eyes, Elbert replied, "There's nothing the fans love more than for me to make a mistake. If I put the ball on the wrong yard line, or somehow miss a call they are all over me. They'll remind me after the game, the next time they see me. And they'll yell at me occasionally, just like they would do at Tubby—only not as much as they did at Tubby, thank goodness! "

Author's note: Other versions of this story appeared in *Out and About* magazine and the University of Delaware *Messenger*.

Geraldine McKeown

Elkton, Maryland

The Artist and Oprah

In the horse country of Cecil County, Maryland, not far from the Pennsylvania line, Geraldine McKeown paints landscapes and still-lifes in a studio standing on land that has been in her family for seven generations, decades before the start of the American Revolution.

When she talks, her description of the area even sounds artistic. "I live at the head of the Chesapeake Bay, where the Tidewater meets the foothills of the Piedmont," she said.

Most of the year, Geraldine works in Maryland. But she also has a summer studio, located in a fishing community on an island in Maine, where, she said, "Magnificent scenery abounds and tourists are few."

Her job is to travel country roads, take photographs, meet interesting people, then return to her studio and capture the essence of a scene with paint and paper. She works alone, sets her own hours, schedules her own deadlines and answers to no one, except herself.

To millions who work a standard 9 to 5 occupation, where they are trapped in meetings and respond to the whims of multiple levels of bosses, Geraldine has a dream job. But, when you add in the fact that she enjoyed a personal meeting with Oprah Winfrey, the envy level of others goes off the chart.

The whole Oprah thing started with the filming of *Beloved*, a 1998 movie that was being filmed in the 5,000-acre Fair Hill Natural Resources Management Area, located near the McKeown property. The film starred Oprah and Danny Glover, and a special movie set was built on the state property.

Because of the attention the filming brought to the area, the Cecil County Chamber of Commerce commissioned Geraldine to paint two original watercolors—one for Glover and one for Winfrey.

"I was very surprised and thought it was a wonderful opportunity," Geraldine said. "I was flattered with the idea and that they invited me to create the paintings."

Working from pictures she took of the movie set, Geraldine painted three originals of the scene, each from a different angle and each reflecting a different season of the year.

The winter scene was for Winfrey, the fall setting for Glover, and the summer painting became a print, and copies are still available.

Creating the paintings is just part of the story. The more memorable event was learning that she was going to present her artwork, in person, to Oprah during the *Beloved* premiere in Philadelphia.

"I was excited and nervous," Geraldine recalled. "Then I had the typical reaction, wondering: 'What do I wear?' and 'What do I say?'"

On Oct. 10, 1998, she and her husband, Bob, and their daughter, Lisa Dolor, traveled to the Four Seasons Hotel. Some people representing the Cecil County Chamber of Commerce also made the trip.

Members of Oprah's staff told Geraldine that the schedule was tight, that they could take pictures and that they should be ready when the star arrived.

Oprah entered the meeting room and, Geraldine said, stayed for about 20 minutes and was very relaxed and very sincere. "She looked at the painting," Geraldine said, "and the first thing she said was, 'I hope you got paid for this.' And I told her I was. She told me she appreciated the work that went into it,

explaining that she had tried working in watercolors and that she knew it was a difficult medium.

"I didn't feel rushed. I was impressed by her sincerity. I feel that the person you see on television is the person she is."

According to an article in the *Cecil Whig* on Oct. 16, 1998, upon seeing her painting, Oprah said, "Fantastic, it's mine. You couldn't have given me a better present." She also told Geraldine, "I admire your talent."

In her 22 years of working as a full-time artist, Geraldine said she considered the meeting with Oprah Winfrey one of her top achievements. The other, she said, occurred in 2003, when her work "Winnowing Basket" was accepted into the American Watercolor Society show, to be exhibited at the Salmagundi Club in New York City.

Over the years, Geraldine's career has been marked by success. Her works have been featured on book covers and in juried exhibitions. She has won best of show medals and critical accolades. Her works have been hung in private homes and in corporate collections. And she has been accepted as a signature member of the National, Baltimore, Philadelphia and Pennsylvania Watercolor societies.

But still, her meeting with Oprah Winfrey seems to resurface from time to time, taking on a life of its own, like an urban legend or local folktale.

"Initially, after it happened," Geraldine said, "people were excited, even more excited than I was. They stopped me and wanted to know, 'Is she like she is on TV?' My reaction is, 'Yes. She's the same type of person.'

"In the Acme checkout, one cashier had heard about me and Oprah Winfrey, and stopped me to talk about it. I didn't even know this person. It was just like she was someone who wanted to be with someone who had been with Oprah. I've become the intermediary between Oprah and John Q. Public. They just seem like they want to touch me. That's a most interesting reaction."

Sometimes, Geraldine said, others have turned her association with Oprah into a part of her biographical description. "When I've been introduced to other people, some will say, 'This is Geraldine. She's an artist, and she met Oprah Winfrey and gave her a painting.' Even after all these years, they still like to say that."

Aside from the accidental combination of events that tossed Geraldine and Oprah together for their brief 20-minute encounter, the Cecil County artist continues her solitary work each day, creating more paintings and prints. Her work setting is both rustic and meaningful. The farm-like building that now serves as her studio was originally a country store, built in 1911 by her great grandfather Gallaher.

She smiled when told most people would love to have her job.

"One of the biggest misconceptions that people have about art," she said,

Geraldine's print of the movie set of Beloved, *built in the Fair Hill Resource Management Area*

"is that you just paint when you want to, and that you have lots of fun. But you have to be disciplined and paint whether you are in the mood or not."

She also said that a serious artist is never away from the work. Whether trying to vacation, travel or relax, the artist's eye is always seeking the perfect scene or evaluating what landscape might be around the next bend.

"It's like your avocation is your vocation," Geraldine said. "You are always at it."

During a recent trip to Ireland with her husband, Bob, she shot 22 rolls of film (36 exposures each). That's material for 792 potential paintings.

"Sometimes I want to close my eyes and stop seeing everything," she said, "because you're always thinking about what will make an interesting painting."

But, the best part of her job, she said, "is when the painting is done, and when you're happy with it. It's a tremendous relief, and you can take a little time off and be a normal person—until the next one."

Is there always a next one?

"Yes," she replied, rolling her eyes.

As we both stood up, concluding the interview, Geraldine paused and walked across the room. Returning a few minutes later, she placed a magazine on a nearby table.

At a special meeting in Philadelphia, Geraldine presents Oprah Winfrey with an original painting of the farm house featured in the movie Beloved.

Photograph by Lisa McKeown Dolor

The artist, perhaps unconsciously captivated by the Oprah connection, had recalled one more incident that had surfaced a few years ago, related to her meeting with Oprah.

"When I met her [Oprah]," Geraldine said, "she told me she was going to hang my painting in her home in Indiana. In the summer of 2001, I was working in Maine, and my daughter, Lisa Dolor, called from Cecil County and said I had to go out and get a copy of the latest issue of *O, The Oprah Magazine*."

Geraldine was able to find the publication at a grocery store and, following her daughter's directions, the artist turned to page 138 of that July 2001 issue. A picture showed Oprah, with guests, seated at a table in the star's farmhouse in Indiana. And, on the wall behind Oprah's chair hangs Geraldine's original painting of the farmhouse from *Beloved*.

"For me," the artist said, "that was the final little nugget that let me know that what she said she meant, and that she had my painting and she was enjoying it. You can imagine all the gifts these people get through the years. That was definitely a highlight for me."

Author's note: For more information on Geraldine McKeown, visit her web site at [www. mckeownart. com].

Adele and Roger Martin at a book signing in Seaford, Delaware

Roger Martin

Middletown, Delaware

Keeping the First State 'First'

When Delaware historians gather to compare facts, trade tales and discuss significant events concerning the First State, the name Roger Martin is certain to enter the conversation.

The Middletown, Delaware, resident is well known in statewide political and professional circles. A former history and foreign language teacher, Roger retired from Middletown High School in 1996, after almost 30 years in the classroom. He left the Delaware General Assembly in 1994, after a 22-year tenure as a member of the Senate, having served twice as majority leader.

Serious Delawareana collectors and students of state history seek Roger's books about the region. They include *A History of Delaware Through Its Governors: 1776-1984* (1984); *Tales of Delaware* (1991); *Delaware's Medal of Honor Winners* (1993); and *Memoirs of the Senate* (1995). *Elbert N. Carvel*, the first of an oral history series on former Diamond State governors published by the Delaware Heritage Commission, was released in 1997; and the sequel, about former Governor Sherman W. Tribbitt was printed in 1998. Never at a loss for ideas, *In Our Midst: Delaware's Vignettes In Pictures and Prose*, Martin's book about interesting local stories and sites, was published in 2000.

My association with "Mr. Martin" began in the early 1960s, when I was a teenage student at Salesianum School and he was my German teacher for two years. I learned about his interest in music when he shared stories about his European singing performances while serving in the U. S. Army.

Over the years, we have met often, usually at

events or programs related to history or politics. So the interview for this book became a combined mini-reunion and an opportunity to catch up on each of our latest plans. We laughed in unison as we compared our long project lists, acknowledging that most of what we hope to accomplish will probably be completed by others years after we've both been planted in Delaware soil.

In the dining room of his home, overlooking a broad expanse of southern New Castle County wetlands, Roger put aside his notebook and pen, turned his back on several half-opened reference books and shared his thoughts about the importance of history, particularly the legacy of his home state.

His interest in the past started in high school when he learned that an ancestor had fought at the Battle of Gettysburg.

"I love history," he said. "There's so much that needs to be shared and that hasn't been done. People forget. Time passes. Many people just don't realize the significance of Delaware's history and the role it played in our country.

"I guess I get the most joy out of it when I uncover things about Delaware's past, and people say, 'I didn't know that!'" he said. "It's important to share our culture and our traditions."

It's also good to be familiar with one's heritage.

"It's extremely important to know your roots," Roger said. "How do you know where you're going if you don't know from where you came? It's sad, really. Today, some people are just adrift, with no sense of their personal or family history. You develop a sense of pride as to who you are, from what your family did, what your folks were and who they were."

He agreed that being a serious historian can be a full-time occupation—and Roger is supported in this endeavor by his wife, Adele. The two met after he came home from the service, while they both were students at the University of Delaware. He frequently mentions his wife's valuable contributions to his writing. As a former English teacher, she reviews his writing and isn't hesitant to make corrections and suggestions.

For the Martins, many an innocent Sunday ride in the country has turned into a quest to uncover buried facts or resolve an unsolved mystery.

"Oftentimes," Roger said, smiling, "I find myself driving down a road and wonder what happened there. I share these thoughts with Adele. I sometimes find myself on back roads, surveying the area, looking at old maps, searching for graveyards, tromping through overgrown bushes."

One of Roger's biggest finds was the grave of John Collins, a 19th-century Delaware governor from Laurel. The long-departed chief executive's resting place had been forgotten for more than a century. The author said he found the gravesite in a family plot in Sussex County that has been grown over and lost from sight.

Another one of his passions is sharing Delaware's importance with others. He said many Delawareans, both native born and transplants, don't know much about the First State's legacy and the important role it played in the founding of our nation.

In a brief, five-minute span of time, he offered a few examples, mentioning the large number of loyal British subjects in southern Delaware at the time of the Revolution; then he touched on the peninsula's importance during the War of 1812; and Delmarva's divided loyalties during the Civil War. He noted the value of the Electoral College to smaller states in the Union; and he closed with an insightful observation on the ever-continuing political, economic and social

If Roger had his way, Delaware Day would be declared a statewide holiday, celebrated with parades, ceremonies and fireworks that resemble a mini Fourth of July.

divisions between residents and politicians on opposite sides of the Chesapeake and Delaware Canal.

With such a strong affection for Delaware, it may surprise some to discover that Roger is not a Delaware native. He was born in 1934 in Delmar, on the Maryland side of the Mason Dixon Line.

"I love Delaware," he said. "I've spent most of my life here. I'm also proud of the fact I'm a Marylander by birth. I've lived in all three counties—mainly in Harrington, Laurel and Newark—so I have an understanding of upstate and downstate."

Smiling, he added, "I know some people in Sussex County who haven't traveled beyond the canal, and they don't intend to. Conversely, in Wilmington, there are some people who don't know anything about Downstate except the beaches."

In such a state as small as Delaware, an outsider might find such divisions surprising, especially when native-born Delawareans constantly flaunt their in-state birth as a status symbol nearly equivalent to owning a two-digit license plate.

Recalling an incident while he was serving in the state legislature, Roger smiled and said one fellow state senator approached him one day with a dead serious look and said, "Seriously, Roger. How much would you pay to be able to have been born in Delaware?"

While traveling throughout the country, Roger also has experienced his share of "Dela-where?" experiences.

"So many people don't know we're a state, or where we're located," he said. "They think it's a place in Texas or in Ohio or in New York. Of course," he added with a smirk, "that doesn't speak too well for the geography departments in their schools."

Regional humor and haughty heritage aside, Roger advocates Delaware claiming its rightful role at the front of the other 49 states.

In a Dec. 17, 2000, column in the Wilmington *News Journal* under the headline "Take a day to hail history," the former state senator makes a case for a statewide commemoration each Dec. 7, which is known as Delaware Day. It marks the First State's ratification of the Constitution in 1787. In Roger's opinion, this date "should be held in high esteem by patriots. It [Dec. 7, 2000] was the 213th anniversary of Delaware's role in starting this great nation.

"You may talk about mighty California and its millions of people, brash Texas, expansive Alaska or big Pennsylvania. None of them can boast like Delaware, that this was the first state."

Pausing to set aside the newspaper, he added, "I don't care how many votes California has. And Pennsylvania, it fooled around and fooled around for too long, and could have ratified the Constitution before we did. But we were first, and that is very important."

If Roger had his way, Delaware Day would be declared a statewide holiday celebrated with parades, ceremonies and fireworks that resemble a mini Fourth of July.

Bringing Delaware's contribution into a contemporary setting, Roger mentioned the recent election between George Bush and Al Gore. The Delaware historian said that the framers of the Constitution knew exactly what they were doing, and insured that voters be treated with a sense of fairness and equality during the presidential election process through the Great Compromise of 1787.

If it weren't for the makeup of the Electoral College, Roger explained, presidential candidates would ignore the smaller states and spend all of their time in population centers, such as New York and California.

But recognition of Delaware Day is only one of Roger's many long-term projects and dreams. Others

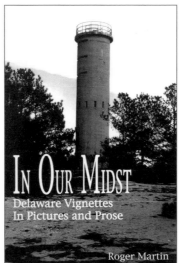

This book features 50 stories and photographs about the First State.

are more immediate, and these literary labors of love sit nearby, patiently waiting for his personal attention.

Working on several books simultaneously fits Roger's style. He said there are numerous cardboard boxes throughout his home—each containing information, leads, notes and assorted documents. He playfully refers to them as "ongoing research in progress."

These plans range from keying into a computer database the names of all taxpaying Delaware residents in 1787, to a personal visit to all the Civil War battlefields where Delaware troops had fought. The complete list is much longer, Roger said. "Actually," he added with a smile, "it tends to grow daily."

While teaching school and serving in the legislature, Roger's creative time was limited. Most of his writing occurred in the summer, on weekends or before or after work. Since he's been retired, one would expect that he'd have more time to enjoy his love of history.

"Well," he said, "a certain portion of my time is taken up by domestic duties, but I do get to work on history every day. And, my wife goes along with it. It's *quid pro quo*. I go with her when she goes shopping and, when we go to a graveyard, she'll sit and read her book."

Of all his professions, Roger seems most comfortable with the label "historian." Ask the prolific writer where he enjoys spending his time and the answer is immediate: "The archives and the library," he said, smiling. "My mouth waters when I think of everything that's there."

Author's note: To contact Roger Martin, send an e-mail note to [RoMar72@aol.com].

Jim Flood Sr.

Dover, Delaware

Delmarva's Newspaper Man

There was a time, only about a generation or two ago—before multi-screen televisions, the Internet, personal computers, cellular telephones and hand-held computer calendars—when daily newspapers were the main source of information in both small towns and big cities. Notice I used the term newspapers—plural—because every big city and most medium-sized towns had more than one daily publication, and some published both morning and afternoon editions.

Competitive reporters tried to scoop their colleagues across town and rushed to be the first to deliver the hot story to old-time editors who chain smoked cigars and kept a bottle of hard stuff in their bottom desk drawer.

But those colorful glory newsdays have gone the way of 19-cent-a-gallon gasoline and Saturday afternoon double features at the neighborhood theater. Today, readers in even major cities find themselves fortunate if they have a single reputable daily paper. Naturally, lack of competition results in a decline of local coverage, fewer human interest features and the loss of long-term reporters who know the region and develop a nose for neighborhood news.

Surprisingly, this need for local news and stories about the milestones and achievements of average folks has been filled in recent years by the small town weekly. Instead of shuttering up their storefronts and melting down their presses, a number of these century-old papers are alive and kicking.

> 'We turn out things that people put in scrapbooks and put on refrigerator doors. We're the record of people's lives and the lives of people they know.'
>
> —Jim Flood Sr.

On the Delmarva Peninsula, several weekly publications are issued by the Dover Post Company, a mini-news dynasty established by Jim Flood Sr., a Maine native and well-respected, long-time Delawarean.

In his second-floor office in the addition to the old hanger that had been part of the original Dover Airfield that opened in 1933—Jim Flood, 75, shared the highlights of his colorful career.

On this summer afternoon, the former administrative assistant to the late Delaware U.S. Senator J. Caleb Boggs, was on the receiving end of an interview, and he seemed to enjoy the opportunity to recall his New England roots and the zigzag route he followed to his present position.

Jim started writing at 16, while in high school in Biddeford, Maine, a blue-collar, New England mill-town. After an injury curtailed his brief football career, Jim began writing sports stories for the *Biddeford Daily Journal*.

"I liked it very much," he said, his soft voice betraying a slight Maine accent that has been modified as a result of his several decades as a resident of Delmarva. "I received 5 cents a published inch. I remember my biggest payday was when I took all the stories I had done over a period of months. I took out a yardstick and measured it and I got $12."

Enlisting in the U.S. Army after high school, Jim said he was able to finagle his way into a job on the Fort Belvoir, Virginia, post newspaper.

"In a twinkling," he said, smiling at the circumstances that still seemed fresh in his mind, "my life was changed from being a basic training recruit. I went down and covered my first story about my own training group with a captain driving me in a Jeep. I was being transported from one level of existence to another."

After his time in the service, Jim said he used that G. I. experience as a stepping stone to work on the college paper while a student at Catholic University in Washington, D. C.

After graduation he decided against following up on a job offer from *Life* magazine; and, from 1952 to 1957, he worked as a reporter and feature writer for the *Baltimore Sun*.

He was assigned to the Eastern Shore, which was connected to the rest of Maryland by the opening of the Bay Bridge in July 1952.

"I opted to go to the hinterland, as opposed to the big city," Jim said. "I preferred the smaller towns. I was hired for the *Sun* and *Evening Sun*. My office was in the Tidewater Inn in Easton. Some of my colleagues considered it a newspaperman's dream, to have a bar and office under the same roof."

Working chiefly in Talbot, Caroline, Queen Anne's and Kent counties, Jim said he escaped from the office quite a bit and got to know the countryside. He also explained that it was beneficial that the parents of his wife, Mary, had a place near Tilghman Island.

Eventually, Jim moved up to Cecil County, working as editor of the *Cecil Whig* for two years, and during that time was involved in starting the weekly *Delaware Sun*. In 1959, Fendall Yerxa, executive editor of the Wilmington *News Journal*, offered him the job of bureau chief in Dover, a new post. Later, following six years on the late U. S. Senator J. Caleb Boggs' staff and six years managing weekly newspapers in Sussex County and nearby Maryland, he and local investors started the Dover Post Company, in April 1975. (Since then, all the non-family members have been bought out.)

Smiling as he recalled the early days of his own newspaper, Jim talked about being involved in the sales, advertising, editorial work, printing and distribution. But, throughout the tough, early years, he said, he and his wife, Mary, with the support of family members, had faith that their business would succeed.

"My accountant," Jim said, shaking his head at the thought, "told me he didn't know how I slept at night. He said I was bankrupt except for the filing."

Now, more than a quarter-century later, the Dover Post Company owns, operates or prints a long list of respected newspapers, including the *Dover Post, Airlifter, Middletown Transcript, Smyrna Clayton Sun-Times, Sussex Countian, Greenville Community News, Hockessin Community News, Mill Creek Community News, Brandywine Community News, Better Years* and *Express*.

Jim Flood's offices and the family's publishing operation have expanded to include more than one site and larger and newer, state-of-the-art presses.

Through his long career, he said, he has followed a significant rule. "On the peninsula, over the

The office of the Middletown Transcript, *established in 1868*

years," Jim remarked, "you keep running into the same people, so you learn not to burn bridges."

There also has been a dedicated effort to deliver and respond to the needs and interests of the communities that the Dover Post papers serve.

"Community newspapers have a very important role in the life of people today," Jim explained, "different perhaps from what it used to be when there weren't the roads that enabled people to travel so easily from town to town. Consequently, in those days, the community paper was supported by the advertising from pretty much the whole business community.

"Now, people are inundated by information from all sides, but it comes down to local news—people reading about news which affects their own community and their own livelihood, which is the weekly's special province.

"Also, it's important to record the things that are milestones in people's lives. They not only see them in print, but they know their friends and neighbors see them in print. This is important, and it's something you don't get with a daily paper, which necessarily has an umbrella coverage of a larger area with many more people involved. A daily has trouble going into as much detail."

He added that a weekly community paper has the advantage of timing. Since it is planned and structured to deliver news and advertising on a weekly basis, busy people still consider the weekly's content as timely, even if they can't get to read it for two or three days. In the case of a daily, if readers get a day or two behind, they are reading old news.

But in his conversation, Jim continually seemed to focus on the needs and habits of his readers—the average, overlooked people that the weekly paper regularly place in the spotlight.

"People," Jim said, "never get so sophisticated, I don't believe, that they ignore what it means to have something in the paper that other people read and then comment to them about."

He also mentioned the milestones of people's lives—births, deaths and marriages.

"But also," Jim said, "the advancement in business, graduation from school, the things that happen to everybody. But when they happen to your family, they take precedence over everything else in the paper."

Recalling a fond memory, Jim illustrated his point. "I remember, a few years ago, I was talking to a fellow in Middletown. I had just met him, and he fished out of his wallet a little clipping, about two inches long, about the time that he had become a member of the volunteer fire company in Middletown. Now that's a story that in the issue of the day did not cause much of a ripple, except to him. He had kept it maybe 30 or 35 years, because he was an older man when I had talked to him. But it had been that important to him.

The Smyrna/ Clayton Sun- Times, established in 1854, is Delaware's oldest continuously operating newspaper.

"Well, that's what we turn out. We turn out things that people put in scrapbooks and put on refrigerator doors. We're the record of people's lives and the lives of people they know."

Reflecting for a moment, Jim talked about the emphasis on "localness." Referring to his editors, he stressed that the defining element of a news story is the local connection, whether or not the information affects that particular community.

"If it's local, it gets attention," he said. "If it isn't local, let somebody else handle it, in some other community. For instance, if the mayor of Dover falls and breaks a leg, it's news. If it happens to the mayor of Wilmington or some other city, it doesn't have a chance of getting in the *Dover Post.*"

Before the end of our conversation, Jim proudly pointed out the strong family connections that have been part of his company from the outset. He talked about his wife, Mary, who was so supportive and worked on the bookkeeping. She still works one day a week on the layout of the *Middletown Transcript.*

As Dover Post Inc.'s chairman of the board and publisher, Jim said that all seven of his children have had some involvement in the family business.

Jim Flood Jr. is current president and general manager of the company;

Mary Flood Kaltreider is in charge of marketing and advertising, along with her husband Fred;

Don Flood is editor of the *Dover Post* and manages the *Middletown Transcript, Smyrna/Clayton Sun-Times* and *Sussex Countian* as well.

David Flood worked for the company in various capacities for 10 years and now, he and his wife, Carolyn, operate their own newspaper in Jim's home town of Biddeford, Maine, along with others in South Portland and Scarborough;

John Flood was editor of the *Middletown Transcript* and is a librarian in the New York public library system;

Ruth Flood worked in the circulation division; and

Paul Flood was editor of the *Middletown Transcript* and *Sussex Countian.*

When asked to select the favorite part of his work, the element of small town newspaper publishing that Jim enjoys the most, he paused. There was a slight crack in his voice. "I just enjoy," he said, softly, "coming into the building in the morning and starting another day. I usually go around and say 'Good morning' to people. It's pretty tough to top that.

"I've been involved in this from the start. At this point, I'm the only one in the company who has been here from day one. I enjoy the people, and I enjoy what I do. I enjoy the writing. I even enjoy the problems; there are always problems. I feel very fortunate to be able to do it. It's a privilege really."

Billy K–Ringmaster

The lights dim. The boisterous crowd, anticipating the start of the legalized rumble, focuses its attention on the center of the elevated ring in St. Matthew's Foley Hall, outside Newport, Delaware.

A short trim man, dressed in a tuxedo and holding a microphone, climbs through the ropes and takes center stage. The glare of spotlights forces several hundred pair of eyes to focus on William Katorkas. On this night, the 49-year-old, University of Delaware police captain once again has been transformed into "BILLY K"—announcer for the East Coast Wrestlers.

For the next few hours, the badge is gone and his FBI Academy training has been placed aside. Katorkas is the main man in the ring, announcing the evening card, sparring verbally and physically with wrestlers three times his size and receiving the abuse and applause of the enthusiastic crowd.

An accidental discovery made during a routine campus investigation in Newark, Delaware, 18 years ago had a dramatic impact on the life of the University of Delaware Public Safety administrator. While taking a report from a student in the Rodney Residence Hall Complex, then-investigator Katorkas noticed several wrestling posters on the student's walls.

During their continuing conversation, Katorkas discovered the student was a professional performer with the East Coast Wrestling Association, and the officer mentioned he might be interested in working as the group's ring announcer.

"I had always been interested in performing, and I always wanted to do announcing," Billy K said, reflecting on the chance meeting in 1984. "My life's dream was to announce an event at the Spectrum. So, I made a few calls, they gave me a tryout and I became the back-up announcer."

Today, Billy K is the main ringmaster at arena-filled events that feature such colorful characters as Boogie Woogie Brown, Cheetah Master, Glamour Boy Lance Diamond, Dr. Destruction and Blue Thunder.

From September through May, the local wrestling group—which was formed by James Kettner and has been headquartered in Elsmere, Delaware, for more than 30 years—performs monthly at St. Matthew's Foley Hall. According to Billy K, approximately 40 wrestlers, ages 21-34, take to the mat for wildly enthusiastic crowds and a regular following of more than 400.

The ring announcer said his attire—a black tuxedo, slicked back hair and gleaming shoes—is a bit

Billy K signs autographs for a fan before the start of the evening wrestling card.

29

Bill Katorkas

Newark, Delaware

conservative when compared to the wild, colorful, flowing garments and props that grace the broad backs of some of his colleagues. However, when he speaks into his microphone, people stop, look and listen.

A veteran of several hundred matches and events, Billy K said he experiences none of the nervousness of his early days. He smiled and admitted that he was "absolutely scared" on the night of his official debut—and being caught in Friday night traffic on I-295 didn't help relax his tension. "I raced into the hall in my tuxedo," he said. "They handed me the match cards and said, 'Good luck!'"

In addition to the pre-match announcing, Billy K is responsible for color commentary, which he provides from a reserved table at ringside.

Such comments as "And the Cheeta Master is going to the high ground!" and "It looks like Cowboy John Blaze is down and out!", delivered in an urgent tone, help get the crowd into the match and heightens their enthusiasm and verbal and physical involvement.

The ring announcer described his role as a combination moderator and cheerleader, who is there to entertain the audience and emphasize the actions of the wrestler-performers.

Time has not diminished Billy K's enthusiasm for his very visible role in the local wrestling world.

"I love it," he said, his smile beaming. "I just like being able to step into somewhat of a fantasy world and act out a childhood dream. This is a role I can fill."

Sometimes, he said, shaking his head, he has met fans in the most unusual places.

"I was in Rehoboth a few years ago, walking down the beach, and this kid says to his mother, 'Look! There's Billy K from wrestling!' I went over and talked to him, told him about the upcoming events. It made him feel good to recognize me, and it made me feel good, too. It's satisfying."

Billy K said he had competed in some high school and college wrestling, but being in the ring with athletes twice his size has provided some interesting moments. He has been slapped, knocked down and tossed airborne across the ring into the ropes. Most of it, he admitted, is part of the show. But, there are those times when things can get a little out of hand.

Seeing the reaction of the crowd tells Billy K that local wrestling shows provide a form of entertainment that people want.

"I like being a part of this," he said. "It's entertainment for a younger audience and for families that don't have the opportunity to afford the big shows or who can't get to Philadelphia."

Police Captain K (by day) and Billy K (at night) said his 15-year-old daughter, Samantha, likes the matches. His twin, 10-year-old sons, Adam and Alex, are absolutely amazed at seeing their father in the ring.

When asked about his most embarrassing moment in the arena, Billy K displayed a small smile and said, "I had started to sing the national anthem, like I do at the beginning of every event, but the tape broke. And I had to finish the entire song by myself. Nobody joined in like I asked them to. It was the longest, most embarrassing moment in my life. I can announce, but I can't carry a tune."

Captain K by day

Ted Stegura

Wilmington, Delaware

Snow Fence Artist

Looking for an interesting way to recycle old odds-and-ends and building materials? Talk to Ted Stegura of Highland West, a development located between Newark and Wilmington, Delaware. All of Ted's original paintings and sculptures are crafted from materials others have discarded and were eager to be rid of.

A big man with a wide smile and infectious laugh, Ted, 71, retired in 1990 after 26 years with Hercules Inc., where he was supervisor of marketing, technical communications and product labeling. While there he was involved in high-tech writing on such complex issues as a final report for the U. S. Advanced Research Project Agency dealing with one of America's first satellites. He said he worked with two engineers who successfully extinguished a burning rocket motor with three gallons of water after previous engineering attempts failed using hundreds of thousands of gallons.

One would expect Ted to slow down but stay involved in writing. He did neither. Instead, he pushed his activities into high gear, and also changed course until he found a creative outlet he enjoyed.

For a while he taught air conditioning and refrigeration repair at Delaware Technical and Community College. Then he got into boating, sailing the Assawoman Bay near his second home in Swan Keys, outside Rehoboth Beach. On an impulse, in early 1993, he tried his hand at art and the creative outlet captured his attention and changed his life.

"Snow fence art" is one of the terms Ted uses to describe his works. His paintings of nature scenes, seascapes and animals are drawn or painted in acrylics on used and discarded pieces of wood—old shutters,

plasterer's wood lathe, floor underlayment, decking materials, treated lumber and construction scraps. He also uses discarded wood for his sculptures and cuts and carves the pieces to frame his paintings.

Since he likes the sea, Ted said, one day he decided to create paintings of a few lighthouses. Liking the results, he tried to make a few sculptured lighthouse models from leftover wood. Today, he has dozens of handmade replicas—some as small as one-foot. Others are taller than six feet, and a special creation graces the front of his Swan Keys getaway.

Among the sculptures in what he calls his "Delaware Collection" are Ted's versions of the Liston Range Front Light, near Port Penn in Bay View Beach; Fourteen Foot Bank Light House (1887), in Bowers Beach; Fenwick Island Light House (1859); Mispillion Light House (1873); Bellevue Rear Range Light House (1909); Reedy Island Rear Range Light House (1908); Delaware Breakwater Light House (1885); Marcus Hook Rear Range Light House (1920); and Cape Henlopen Light House (first built in 1765, destroyed in 1926).

Ted's also created sculptures of out-of-state structures—including Portland Head Light in Maine, Assateague Light in Virginia, Highland Light in Cape Cod and the Thomas Point Light near Annapolis.

"I look at a poster and I start building it," Ted said. "I go through trial and error until each piece fits."

Each smaller-sized finished sculpture is made primarily of wood and rests on a finished base, which reflects the setting where the sculpture is located. This can be the seashore, marshland or a developed suburban area. Some of his later, larger pieces are of molded concrete.

Ted said he attempts to make the lighthouses as close as possible to the original. But he saves no plans and keeps no templates of the model's measurements. When he creates a second piece of the same subject—which is rare—it will never be an exact duplicate.

"If I do a second piece," he stressed, "it's different to some degree. And that's what makes each piece original, a one-of-a-kind piece of art."

Ted has visited the sites of many of his lighthouses and he's done extensive library research on each building. This is reflected in the historical plates he attaches to each sculpture. These provide information on the background of the particular light, plus details on its date, original construction and other details.

Standing over his replicas of two black-metal towers, Ted pointed out subtle differences based on his readings. Like an historian, he casually shared construction information on the screwpile lights on the Chesapeake Bay and the caisson watertight bases used to erect several lights in the lower Delaware Bay.

One of Ted's lighthouse creations on his deck in Swan Keys

Other projects, he said, aren't supposed to be exact replicas.

"Many of my nautical scenes, I do differently," he said. "I'll get an idea in my head. I visualize what it should be, and then I start to building. I add from memory and from photographs. It's not totally exact, but then it's not supposed to be. Often, I build as I go along. I have no idea what it will look like when I'm finished.

"Sometimes, I'm amazed at this entire career, since it occurred totally by accident," Ted explained. "I'm self taught. I painted a few sea pigeons and the work turned out pretty good, and then I just kept going. That was eight years ago, and now I'm into a dozen different areas at once."

Some of his work is a combination of painting and sculpture. He's salvaged discarded coffee tables—including one special find of solid maple—and he has carved or burnt nautical scenes into the tops.

Those interested in making sure they have one of Ted's creations should seek out his distinctive "Teddy Bear" signature.

"That's me," Ted said, "I'm 'Teddy Bear.' A few friends and I were at the racetrack, and they were fooling around and gave me the name and it stuck."

Unlike commercial artists, Ted doesn't do any market testing or attempt to satisfy a large range of potential buyers.

"I just do it!" he said. "I don't care if it sells or not. I've got a house full of it. I got a garage full of it. I get attached to my own work. But I will make something special if someone asks for it."

Smiling, Ted admitted he's quite satisfied when his buyers are pleased with his work and ask for more.

"When they like it," he said, "I feel good. I sometimes think I can do better, 'cause I know my own mistakes, see things that other people don't. Like I said earlier, I like to do things once."

Ted spoke proudly of his special Teddy Bear guarantee. "My buyers accept my custom-built work only if they are satisfied," he said. "That means, I

tell them they only pay me if they like it. If they don't like it, I'll keep it. And I mean it. "

When asked if he would like to get an order to do 20 sculptures of the same lighthouse, Ted frowned.

"No! " he said without hesitation, almost shouting the reply. "That would be work. That would be torture. I don't enjoy making the same thing more than once. "

Cecilia, Ted's wife of over 40 years, smiled when discussing her husband's full-time, second career. "He surprised me, " she said. "He surprised us all. "

"Hell! " Ted interjected, "I surprised myself! " Then Teddy Bear added, "She wouldn't let me sell the lighthouse we have out at Swan Keys. "

"It's beautiful, " Ceil said, agreeing. "But all of his work is good, " she said, proudly. "It keeps him real busy. He's always out in the back working, and I can come and go as I please. But he doesn't do what he needs to do in the house. He's out playing in the shed until the very last minute. "

Standing outside his workshop, affectionately named the "Shed House, " Ted showed off some of the diverse tools of his trade—construction foam, a metal sewer cap, a plastic flower pot, some discarded children's toys, broken pieces of snow fence and a brass urn. All of them, he said with conviction, would eventually contribute to some piece of Teddy Bear artwork.

"I do three, four things at one time, " he said. "I'm building my ship model, putting final decorations on a lighthouse while waiting for masonry to dry on another one, or I'll be making a few simple plaques. I don't like to wait on anything. I can't take a rest. "

Pausing, Ted said, with a smile while shaking his head, "At one time, I thought I had a great idea. I figured that I might build every lighthouse in the United States. Then I read a book on lighthouses of Maine, and I found out there were at least 200 working lights in that state alone. That killed that idea real quick. "

But then there are dozens of other projects calling out to Teddy Bear: Lighthouses of his "Chesapeake

Bay Collection, " a model of the *USS Fremont* APA-44, the ship on which he sailed while in the Navy, more pieces of snow fence art, a few seven-foot-tall lighthouses for neighbors in Swan Keys, orders for his popular shantytown and fishtown wall sculptures, a few dozen nautical plaques, a mural or two and, of course, whatever else might catch his eye along the way.

Ted mentioned that another of his favorite creations sits on a shelf, overlooking his bed at his home near the Delaware shore. "It's an exact replica of *Jenny*, the dilapidated shrimp boat that appeared in the Oscar-winning movie *Forrest Gump*. You see, I work on whatever catches my fancy, and I enjoy doing it. "

I smiled, then said that for those who are not fortunate enough to enjoy the fruits of retirement, Ted's life sounds like a dream come true.

Looking at me for a moment, he shook his head and nodded. Then he tossed out one of his deep Teddy Bear laughs and added, "If I'm bored, I'll go out back in the Shed House and start a project. I don't know what the hell it's gonna be. But it will be something. That's the life. "

You're right, Ted. That's the life.

Author's note: Contact Ted Stegura at (302) 998-2470.

An assortment of Ted's snow fence art

Joe Smolka and Billy Shutt

Newport, Delaware

Birthday at the Grammys

Billy Shutt didn't expect to spend his 15th birthday out of town. He thought he'd go to school, have a little party at the house, share cake with the relatives and open a few presents—maybe get a few CDs, some video games and clothes. Every growing teenager needs clothes.

But his uncle, Joe Smolka, 58, had bigger plans—much bigger plans. He decked himself and Billy out in tuxedos, bought Amtrak tickets to the Big Apple and took his nephew to Madison Square Garden to see the 45th annual Grammy Awards—live and in person.

I had known Joe since we were students in Wilmington's St. Hedwig's Elementary School in the 1950s. We grew up in the same Polish neighborhood, living in row houses only a block apart. Joe played the saxophone and clarinet. I played the trumpet. In the 1970s and '80s, we performed together in the Golden Bells, a polka and wedding band.

It was during the days when we were on the road, playing in clubs and dance halls from Baltimore to northern New Jersey, that Joe started producing record albums. At first they were 33-1/3 vinyl LPs. Later, he moved into cassettes and CDs.

As a result, he was accepted as a voting member of the National Academy of Recording Arts & Sciences, the prestigious organization that conducts balloting for the annual Grammy Awards. And for the last 15 years, he has voted in the four major categories: for best record, album and song of the year, plus best new artist.

However, he also is eligible to vote in eight of the 28 specialized categories. In 2003, Joe submitted his ballot in polka, world music, children, country and gospel categories.

"Usually, the awards ceremony is held in Los Angeles," Joe said. "When it came to New York this year, I decided I was going to go. Since I am allowed to purchase two tickets, I planned to take someone along."

Since Billy's birthday was Feb. 24 and the Grammy awards ceremony was Feb. 23, a few months before the event Joe began hinting to his nephew that he might be going to New York City for his birthday.

In early February, Billy said, his Uncle Joe gave him the good news. "I was excited," Billy recalled. "He said he ordered the tickets. We told my whole family that we were going. I think my sisters—Angie and Bernadette—were a little jealous. Then he made arrangements to rent us tuxedos."

A pair of highly desired tickets to the Grammy Awards

The uncle and his nephew boarded a train on Sunday morning and headed for the Big Apple to experience behind-the-scenes action and antics that few of the millions of television viewers are even aware of.

The academy doesn't send the tickets in the mail, Joe explained. He received a special voucher that had to be redeemed, in person, at the Sheraton on Seventh Avenue New York Hotel and Towers. This prevents scalping, theft or sale on the Internet of the sought-after reserved tickets.

The duo's first objective was to attend the 4:30 p.m., pre-telecast awards ceremony in Madison Square Garden. Joe said this presentation program is for the winners of the lesser-publicized categories. While standing in line to enter the building, Joe and Billy met the man who makes the Grammy statuettes.

"His name is John Billings and he's from Colorado, and he was wearing this big cowboy hat," Joe said. "When he told me what he did, I asked him

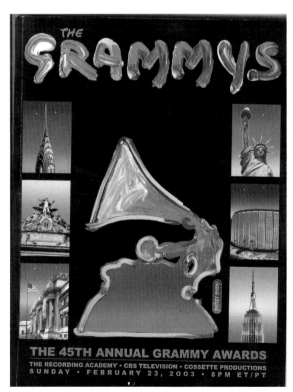

The official program for the 2003 Grammy Awards ceremonies

for one of the little Grammy statues. But he said he couldn't even sell me one, because each one is registered and they're very strict about the production and security with them."

Because there were only about 1,600 people at the late afternoon event, Billy and Joe had excellent seats near the front row, just below the stage.

"We were sitting with record producers, artists, all the award winning acts," Joe said.

"I couldn't believe it," Billy said. "I was sitting next to a Grammy winner, and there were more behind me, all around us. Norah Jones, who would win eight Grammys that night, came to the afternoon ceremony. We were really close to where she was standing. It was like a dream. It was just amazing to be there and experience it."

Laughing, Joe added, "This guy behind me jumps up and shouts out, 'Hey! I won a Grammy!' I mean, I'm touching this guy. I didn't know who the hell he was and what he won, but he was happy. But after each of them got their awards, they went to the back of the hall for photos and interviews. After a while, as the seats were emptying, we were the only ones who didn't get awards."

One of the surprises of the night, Joe and Billy agreed, was the discovery of "seat fillers." Joe explained that a group of young and attractive men and women, many with exotic names like Carlos, Suretta and Natasha, go online a few days before major televised events and sign up to fill empty seats. This insures a full house and the seat fillers enjoy the performance and sometimes are invited to after-show parties.

Joe said that 85 percent of the more than 20,000 attendees were dressed in either tuxedos or expensive gowns. "The women," Joe added, "were dressed to kill."

"We spent a lot of time looking at the women," Billy recalled with a smile.

During the evening program, Billy and Joe enjoyed performances and appearances by such stars as Simon and Garfunkle, Bruce Springsteen, Bono,

Alan Jackson, Vanessa Carlton and Eminem. But the highlight of the trip, Joe said, was the afternoon presentation of a Grammy to the Blind Boys of Alabama in best traditional soul and gospel category.

"That was the most memorable moment of the day," Joe said. "Getting the Grammy was the next best thing to God coming down for them. You could see through their body motion how excited they were. I was crying when I saw that."

The two travelers arrived home on Monday morning, about 5 a.m., and Billy took his birthday off to rest up from the trip. On Tuesday, when he returned to school, he casually mentioned where he had been.

Of course, no one believed him.

"I was talking to this girl, Kelly, about what I did over the weekend and I said, 'I went to the Grammys.' I could tell she didn't believe me. She just gave me that disbelief look and smiled and said, 'Yeah. Right.' Then I started telling my whole class, but no one believed me. I didn't have any pictures, because you weren't able to take a camera inside.

"The following day, I brought in the program, and we had pictures of us in tuxedos that were taken before we left. Some of my friends talked to my Mom and she told them that I went there. Then they slowly started to believe me."

When asked why he decided to take Billy to the ceremony, Joe said, "I figured he knew the different groups and that he would enjoy the experience 20 times more than I would." Laughing, he added, "He's my security guard. I wanted to go to New York and I decided this was his birthday present, and his high school graduation present and college present and marriage present and first-born present.

"I also wanted to see the process. It was exciting to be in the building and watch what goes on during a live program. I would go again, but I would do it just to take someone else to see their reactions."

Finding someone to accompany him seems the least of Joe's problems.

"I have a lot of nieces and nephews," Joe said, smiling. "So I will probably work up the age scale. I have two waiting in the wings. Connor and Casey said they want to go next. Plus, there are other people who have found out that I went and they keep hinting around, asking what it was like to be at the Grammys and if I need a friend to go with me, they're available. I've even got people I never met before asking me if I've got an extra ticket for next year."

Besides the excitement of attending a major musical event, Joe said there is something special about the Grammys.

"There are so many music awards," he said. "But the most famous, the very top one, is the Grammys. When a famous musician or singer dies, they always put in the obituary how many Grammys that person has won.

"Being a member of the academy is an honor," Joe added. "It's a relatively small group that get to vote on these recordings. Out of all of the organizations I belong to, it's the top. People take the Grammys seriously."

More than 40 years separate Billy and his Uncle Joe, but the difference in age is no barrier to their friendship and mutual interests. They attend baseball games, go on walks and have a weekly night out eating wings at their favorite restaurant.

"We have a good time together," Billy said. "We always enjoy ourselves and get into trouble. We both laugh and, in a good way, we make fun of ourselves and of other people. And we always meet interesting characters."

Joe nodded, and then added, "He really hangs out with me because I pay for everything. He's also my godchild, and we try to enjoy each moment and we enjoy doing things together.

"He's not going to be with me forever. When he gets that first girlfriend, that's going to be it. So maybe for his 16th birthday we'll go to the Grammys one more time. But only if it's in New York."

Photograph by Jerry Rhodes

Eddie Okonowicz

Middletown, Delaware

Searching for Gold in the Ground

When you talk about treasure hunting, most people think of digging up pirate loot on deserted islands, or finding old chests filled with gold, silver and jewelry, often protected by sharks and giant squids that prowl the watery realms of Davy Jones' locker.

But Delaware native and long-time treasure hunter Eddie Okonowicz sees things differently. He knows that wherever people have been—where they have lived, played and worked—something has been left behind. In fact, he says as much in his book on the subject, *Treasure Hunting: Seek and You Shall Find.*

Eddie has been seeking and finding all manner of buried treasure ever since he first starting digging holes in his parents' back yard as a six-year-old.

Within a couple of years, he was the proud owner of a beginner-level metal detector. By the time he was in high school, he had moved up to the top of the line, a White's metal detector.

"I saw a newspaper article about a guy in north Wilmington named Harry Bodofsky," Eddie said. "I brought my first metal detector from him."

Since then, Eddie, who works as a cancer research nurse in the Christina Care Health System, has upgraded his metal detector at least four times.

In the early days, digging around in the back yard of his parents' home near Newport, the treasures consisted mostly of rusty screws, nails and soda can pull tabs—but you have to start somewhere.

With the purchase of the White's metal detector, Eddie sought new places to explore, and it was about this time that his efforts began to pay off.

"I went into the local park and did some treasure hunting there," Eddie said. "It was there that I started to find coins from the 1940s and upwards."

While his quest for buried treasure has taken him from the First State to Maryland, Pennsylvania, Virginia and North Carolina, Eddie said that each place offers its own kind of reward.

Besides exploring the family yard, Eddie has found that schools, woods, campgrounds and parks also have a lot to offer those who are patient and follow the rules of responsible hunting and good citizenship.

"Each state has different restrictions, and the rules in state and county parks can vary, so be aware of these restrictions before hunting," Eddie said. "On schools, always hunt on weekends or after regular school hours—and always get permission."

While beaches are another lucrative choice for treasure hunters, Eddie's favorites are the open spaces, and in particular, plowed fields.

"When people go treasure hunting, a lot of them will go to a local school or park," Eddie said. "They might find anywhere from a couple of dozen to over 50 coins in one outing, but rarely will they find something of value."

And that, Eddie says, is why hunting in plowed fields and other sites (again, always with permission) is the most rewarding.

"In most areas, like your yard, coins sink about one inch every 10 years, so that means if you locate a coin five inches down, it should be about 50 years old," Eddie said. "In plow fields, which are turned over once every year, you can discover just about everything."

It is in farm fields that Eddie finds most of his valuable items, such as a 200-year old coin that was in an area where a church and a home had once stood.

In order to make such discoveries, Eddie said you have to know what was originally in the area, to get a feel for the kinds of treasure you might find.

Some of the most helpful sources of information, he said, are libraries, where you can consult books, newspapers and maps. A valuable research method, Eddie added, is talking to the elderly, who are glad to have an opportunity to share their experiences about an area where they grew up or have lived all their lives.

"I look at old maps, to see where taverns and homes were located," Eddie said. "When I go treasure hunting, I look for signs like brick fragments and pottery shards, to see if families may actually have lived there."

One of the most rewarding sites was a 300-acre field near Bear, Delaware, which had been sold by the owner and was awaiting development by a local contractor. The owner gave Eddie permission to treasure hunt 20 acres of what had been a soybean field. On this site, Eddie believes he found what might have been a mitten—a dump used by people in rural areas before the advent of regular trash collections became a part of modern day living.

"They would throw broken dishes and other items in this site," Eddie said. "This field produced over 400 items, including coins from 1780-1850, and 16 U.S. Navy uniform buttons that dated back to the War of 1812."

Eddie also found a "pearl ware" sugar bowl that

Treasure Hunting Seek and You Shall Find

EDDIE OKONOWICZ

was probably made during the mid-18th century in England.

"We found pieces of ceramic about three feet underground, and we were able to glue them back together," Eddie said. "The sugar bowl came from Straffordshire, England, and probably fell off somebody's table more than 200 years ago. We would never have found it if we had not been digging there."

He and his associates also get calls from people who want them to bring a metal detector to find a metal item that has been lost in someone's yard.

"There are stories of wives throwing their wedding rings out the window and the husband getting a friend with a detector to try to recover the jewelry," he said, smiling.

Of course, Eddie said, this is just a single example of some of the wonderful stories that are shared by other treasure hunters. When they get together, the conversations are much like those of fishermen—exaggerating the tale of the treasure that was almost found, the gold in the ground that got away . . . for the time being.

"Treasure hunting is serious business," Eddie said, mentioning people who have invested thousands of dollars in expeditions to find the booty in local shipwrecks and pirate treasure along the Delaware coastline.

Has anyone found anything significant?

Smiling, Eddie replied, "Of course we always do. But we may not tell you about it, at least not right away."

Although his wife, Karen, has no interest in treasure hunting, Eddie said they both enjoy history and items from bygone times.

Among his favorite finds are items from the Civil War, the War of 1812 naval buttons, coins from the 1600s to mid 20th century, as well as pottery, jewelry and religious items.

One thing Eddie has not found is a gold coin, but that does not mean he is going to stop trying.

"I'm still going to look for that elusive gold coin," Eddie said. "You never know when it will turn up."

Although he recommends that serious treasure hunters rent a safety deposit box at a bank for security reasons, he does on occasion share his findings with others during presentations he gives at local libraries and nursing homes.

"I like looking back and identifying what I have found. It is a chance to hold on to history," Eddie said. "When I do a presentation, it gives others a chance to do the same thing and to share my experiences."

Perhaps the most rewarding part of the whole experience, Eddie said, is spending time outdoors, away from the demands and distractions of modern life.

"And," he said, "I usually don't go home empty handed."

—Jerry Rhodes

Just a few of the relics collected over the years from backyards, farm fields and playgrounds

Assorted display of various items.

Photograph by Jerry Rhodes

Neighbors

Photograph by Kathy F. Atkinson

Dean Rice

North East, Maryland

Caring for Charlie

Each town has its very own cast of characters and celebrities. Usually, they are recognizable persons who have endeared themselves to the community because of an impressive record of good deeds. Others may stand out because of their unique dress or quirky habits. And some are noticed simply because they have been around the area longer than anyone else.

In North East, Maryland, a tiny watertown on the upper reaches of the Chesapeake Bay, "Charlie," one of the area's better known figures, is still out and about, making the rounds. However, there are two interesting facts that non-area residents must realize. Charlie is a goose, and he has not been seen in these parts for several years.

Dean Rice, 78, a retired industrial arts teacher from North East High School, and community leader, said that from the mid 1970s until about 1992, Charlie roamed the shipyards, parks, private lawns and shores of the upper bay the entire year.

Essentially, North East was his turf, Dean said.

Believed to be a large, white Snow Goose, no one knew where Charlie came from or exactly when he first appeared. But set down roots the friendly goose did.

Over the years, Charlie was adopted by people in the area. Tourists and seasonal residents, who came down for the summer, would feed Charlie off their boats. Townspeople, both adults and children, would

> *'I guess I feel I'm doing a service to the county and community, by bringing back something they enjoy. He's just an old friend, and not just of mine. He's an old friend of a lot of people.'*
>
> *—Dean Rice*

toss him food. Whether Charlie happened to be roaming the town park or strolling on a private lawn he was recognized and never mistreated.

Boatyard workers knew Charlie and watched out for him. And, Dean added, there were people who would come down every day from Rising Sun, Maryland, about 12 miles away, just to feed him.

"Oh, Charlie," Dean said, with a sigh, you could almost see him creating a memory in his mind, "he was very special. He really was."

So if Charlie is gone, how did Dean get him back?

In 1981, Eileen Leake, an artist whose husband was stationed at nearby Aberdeen Proving Ground, lived in the area. She saw the white goose and created a large oil painting on a canvas, 6 feet tall and 4 feet wide.

According to Dean, she was so proud when it was completed, and she told her landlord that she had just painted "Mother Goose."

"But," Dean added, "her landlord said, 'That's not Mother Goose! That's Charlie!'"

The painting was displayed in Betty's Studio Gallery on Route 40, but it never sold. Several years later, when the Army transferred the artist's husband to California, the painting of "Charlie" went out West with the family.

At that time, Charlie still roamed the area and had an ever-increasing following, Dean said.

Through correspondence between Leake and North East mail carrier Bobbi Elko, Dean learned that the painting of Charlie was still available. Since the goose was missed by many folks in the area, Dean sent a letter to Leake inquiring about its purchase.

The artist agreed to sell "Charlie" for $500, and Dean started a grassroots effort to secure the funds. Through word- of- mouth, local newspaper stories and the cooperation of merchants, citizens and area clubs the money was raised.

"Charlie" returned to North East in the summer of 1995.

Since then, Dean has been organizing the painting's travel-ing tour. He placed "Charlie" in such public sites as the First National Bank of North East, County Bank, Colonial Florist, England's Colony on the Bay, Woody's Crab House, Calvert and Elk Neck elementary schools and other area sites.

Dean Rice stands beside Charlie, while the painting was on display in the Upper Bay Museum in North East, Maryland.

On the day of the interview, Charlie dominated one wall of the Upper Bay Museum. "I don't know where he's going next," Dean added. "Somebody will ask for him. One lady wanted to buy him and put him over her fireplace. Several people want him. But I think he belongs to the town of North East."

Listen to Dean and he readily spins tales of dozens of incidents, each one associated with a fond memory of the goose he still calls "his friend."

There was the time that the news camera crew came down from Baltimore television, Dean said. They were talking to Miss Ellen Cantler, a town resident who lives on the river. They asked her about the area geese, saying they'd like to get some pictures.

"She told the reporters, 'I'll call them,'" Dean recalled, "and the reporters laughed at her. 'Charlie! Charlie!,' she yelled. And he came a running. They have it on video. They couldn't believe it."

Charlie was a leader of other water-fowl who had settled in the area. "He supervised the crip-pled geese," Dean said. "He'd honk and they would all come to life, follow him everywhere.

"He was sure something. I guess the funniest thing I ever saw was calling him in off the ice, and there were lots of other geese and mallard ducks following him. They were all falling and slipping and sliding all over the place."

Dean said Charlie was important enough to be featured on the program cover of the North East Water Festival one year, was often pictured in local

newspapers and written up and pictured in the *Shoreman* magazine.

No one knows for sure where Charlie came from. Dean thinks he may have been somebody's pet. As far as Dean can tell, the goose's name came about when Dean was in his front yard and heard a girl calling "Charlie! Charlie!" and the goose responded.

As best as he can determine, Dean said Charlie's 20-year reign as a local character ended about 1992.

Unfortunately, Dean said, years ago everybody in town knew about Charlie. Now, with newcomers and the passing of time, fewer people are familiar with his old friend's story.

That may be part of the reason that Dean continues to find Charlie's traveling portrait a home after all these years.

"When you get my age, you do what you do to keep active. It's fun, and Charlie, he was my friend."

One wonders what will happen to Charlie when Dean is no longer around to coordinate the painting's year-round local tour.

"The older I get, the longer it takes to move him around," Dean admitted. "He's liable to be where I left him. He might end up here in the museum or some elementary school. Someone will have the ambition to take him."

For now, that's not Dean's concern. Quietly, every few weeks, he continues to find a place for Charlie's safekeeping, for a month, a few weeks, however long they'll have him. Then, alone, Dean takes down the huge portrait, packages it carefully, loads it into his vehicle and heads for the next receptive host.

And when Charlie's time is up, Dean will move him again . . . and again . . . .

"The last time I saw him," Dean said, slowly, remembering their final meeting, "the sparkle was gone out of his eyes. He had a hole in his foot. We didn't expect to see him much longer. Nobody knows where Charlie went off to die. I guess he's back here in the swamp somewhere. Nobody ever found him after he disappeared.

"I guess I feel I'm doing a service to the county and community, by bringing back something they enjoy. He's just an old friend, and not just of mine. He's an old friend of a lot of people."

Bob Chance

Darlington, Maryland

Bigfoot in Maryland?

For decades stories about Bigfoot, North America's version of the Himalayan Abominable Snowman, have appeared at irregular intervals in supermarket tabloids—and in some more reputable newspapers and magazines.

While a vast majority of the sightings of the mysterious creature since the early 1900s have occurred in the Pacific Northwest, there have been some reports of hairy, ape-like Sasquatch beings in other areas of the United States. Interestingly, more than a few unexplained footprints and, in a some cases, unsubstantiated reports have occurred in the state of Maryland.

Bob Chance, 56, is an environmental scientist, naturalist, Greenway Trail manager and former high school science teacher from the Darlington area of Harford County, Maryland. In 1972, he stumbled upon a possible Bigfoot incident. Since that time, Bob has been involved in researching scores of incidents in the Delmarva area of eastern Maryland related to the nocturnal, barrell-shaped, ape-like creature.

We sat in the studio of Bob's historic colonial-era home, in the quaint Village of Berkley, surrounded by arrowhead displays, colorful turtle shells, framed butterflies, stuffed owls, tropical fish, an extensive natural science library and photographs from his travels on other continents. At a thoughtful, relaxed pace, the soft-spoken founder and former director of the Susquehannock Environmental Center shared some of the more unusual experiences that have occurred during 30 years of investigation.

In the spring of 1972, Chance was leading a high school canoe trip in Muddy Creek, Pennsylvania, on the Susquehanna River about 15 miles north of his home.

One of the canoes had gotten lodged under a waterfall, and he and several students spent some time recovering it from the rocky gorge. Close to sunset, as the group was walking back to the truck through the forest, a 30-lb. rock landed in front of them. It came from the ridge above. Soon, another rock of similar size and weight landed nearby, Bob recalled. One of the rocks struck a student in the shoulder, and the teacher and the rest of the party shouted at the unseen assailant.

Racing to the top of the ridge, the group sensed that an animal or person was very close. They decided to take the injured student to the hospital rather than pursue their attacker. But, as they traversed the opposite hillside toward the truck another rock was tossed in their direction.

Bob said he wondered who or what may have tried to harm them . . . or keep them away. At first, he thought it probably was a human, or maybe a buck that had accidentally dislodged the rocks as it ran across the ridge.

About 18 months after the rock throwing incident, while attending a conference on the Sasquatch, Bob discovered a possible answer. The conference participants discussed the secretive creature's tendency to throw things, at irregular intervals, in the direction of those who approached.

"I didn't know much about the creature's habitat or behavioral pattern at the time," Bob said. But he discovered that at other sightings the animal had been known to throw things at intruders.

Over the years, his interest in Bigfoot continued,

and he periodically visited isolated watersheds throughout Harford County, checking out reports of unexplained incidents.

Being called to examine a trail of very large footprints in the snow during the winter of 1978 near Delta, Pennsylvania, increased Bob's belief that there might be a mid-Atlantic version of Bigfoot in Maryland.

By the late '70s, Bob said he had investigated—in person or by phone—more than 20 sightings. At that time, combining what he had learned with the subsequent incidents, Bob began to think that the rock throwing incident that had occurred years earlier in Muddy Creek may have been caused by a passing Sasquatch.

As of early 1996, his slim folder had grown to contain 104 incidents, most in a 25-mile radius of his home. Generally, his area of research extends from the Gunpowder Falls in the southwest to Muddy Creek in the north, Deer Creek and Broad Creek in the south and the Octorara region in Cecil County to the east.

"I've talked to coon hunters and farmers, hikers and deer hunters," he said. "They've told me of hearing screams, strong odors, huge tracks and missing livestock. Over the years, I've gotten a sense of what the animal's feeding patterns are, plus its intelligence, curiosity and its instinctive ability to avoid detection."

After talking with other researchers in different parts of the world, including British Columbia and Washington State, Chance developed a list of factors that would make it difficult, or even impossible, for Bigfoot to exist in the East. These include: the dense population, lack of a large undeveloped/forested area and topography that did not help concealment.

"I wondered why one of the creatures hadn't been wounded by a car or sighted by deer hunters or seen going through peoples' garbage. Even if it's nocturnal, there should be someone who has seen one. I'm still wondering about these things. Even though I've never seen it, I still can't stop the quest."

Never far from Bob's thoughts are the tracks. It always seems to come back to markings in the snow. Similar to the Delta, Pennsylvania, footprints in 1978, significant sets of very large tracks appeared in the winter of 1995.

A sudden February snowfall provided evidence of a very large creature that seemed to travel the length of Harford County, as it headed from southeast to northwest into nearby Pennsylvania. During that excursion through the area, Bob said, at least six families reported finding footprints of some kind. Some of those people also reported seeing a large creature near their farms or homes during that single winter evening.

Remnants of the tracks indicated a three-toed creature with 15-inch feet with up to a 70-inch stride.

"I hadn't much to go on for about 10 years," Bob said. "That series of events was quite significant."

Bob admitted that, over the years, he has earned himself a reputation as the area's foremost Bigfoot hunter. Telephone calls to his home reporting unusual incidents are not uncommon. In addition to footprints, people have reported high-pitched shrieking.

"They've been described as wails with various levels of amplitude," Chance said. "I've heard the sounds, in the outdoors and on tape recordings. It's almost like a shrill whistle, but it can end in a roar. It's as if it comes from a chest cavity of tremendous proportions."

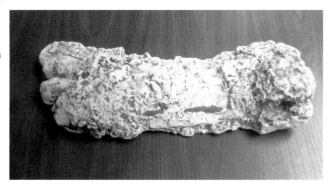

A plaster cast of a three-toed track found behind rocks on Sharon Acres Road in 1975

In 1977, in Deer Creek Valley, Bob said a woman discovered large tracks in her garden. One night, all the dogs in the neighborhood charged out after the unseen monster. One dog never returned. It was found swinging from a tree, 10 feet above the ground with its neck broken.

"Most dogs cower in fear from the scent," said Chance. "It's like sewage or sulfur or rotten eggs. I've heard it described as smelling like rotting meat. Some say it emits an odor when harassed or approached, like a skunk."

In a few instances, witnesses have told the Maryland Bigfoot hunter they've noticed the creature staring in house windows, apparently fascinated with the passing images on televisions. Bob said he has read reports that similar traits have been displayed by gorillas in zoos.

He smiled as he mentioned that he gets some odd looks when strangers realize he has more than a passing interest in Bigfoot. The reaction can range from aloofness and ridicule to a desire to accompany him on the hunt.

"A lot of people want to be in on the actual research," he said. "I practically always turn them down. Some of them have actually seen something themselves, and they want reinforcement in their own minds. But I usually go alone, with a tape recorder and camera. Sometimes I take my dogs. The more people involved reduces the chances of an encounter, since the animal can sense the intrusion."

In two instances, Bob believed he had been close to an encounter with the creature of his quest. One

was near a garbage dump behind a trailer close to Deer Creek.

"I pulled down the driveway at dusk," he recalled. "I heard tremendous thrashing. Whatever it was ran right through the tree saplings at a high rate of speed. The next day, I returned and took some plaster casts of the footprints.

> *'I'm a dreamer. I'd like to think that not everything on the planet has been categorized, that there's still some pocket of natural history and wildness that hasn't yet been discovered.*
>
> *'It might be there. It might not be there. It may be a bogus fairy tale I'm tracking, but I think not. Sometimes, I find myself thinking that, in the future, someone will find this thing and say, "That thing Chance was talking about 25 years ago is really out there."'*
>
> *—Bob Chance*

"People ask me if I've ever been scared, and my answer is 'Yes.' I was definitely scared when rocks, double the size of a football, were being thrown.

"Still, I'll go into abandoned stone shells or ruins that used to be barns or homes. I have this image of the animal, standing flush against the wall in the darkness. I don't think it will hurt me. I hope it realizes I'm not aggressive and mean no harm."

After reviewing more than 100 local reports, Bob said he has some opinions on the possible physical characteristics of the creature:

· Nearly 7 feet tall, weighing 350-500 lbs.
· Extremely long arms
· Sloped cranium
· Barrel chest
· Very large mid section
· No neck
· Flat nose
· Reddish to brown to salt-and-pepper hair

And regarding its habits:

· There are significantly fewer, probably 100 to 200, in the Eastern corridor than the larger numbers estimated to be in the West,

· They travel in three- or five- member groups or, in the case of males, alone, like African mountain gorillas,

· A half- dozen use the corridor through Harford County going north in summer and south in winter,

· They winter in the lower Appalachians (places like Alabama, northern Georgia and central Florida),

· They do not stay in one particular habitat and have learned to keep moving,

· They follow the ancient migratory routes of the elk, moose, deer and bear,

· They follows the river valleys and the steep slopes of the Piedmont and

· They are omnivorous, feeding opportunistically on meat and vegetation.

Bob admitted that his greatest fear is that with more publicity about its presence, a trophy hunter in an all- terrain vehicle would be thrilled to mount the carcass on the hood and do severe disservice to scientific study.

After nearly three decades, one may wonder why Bob continues his search. After all these years, does he have an objective, a focus, something he would like to achieve?

"I want to prove the animal does exist," he said, "through photos or by witnesses' accounts. If it could be captured, I'd want to sedate it, examine it and let it go, perhaps with a radio transmitter.

"The activity seems to come irregularly," Bob said. "The follow- up doesn' t take much out of me. I'll go years with nothing and then, all of the sudden the calls come in. I can' t establish a pattern, but that's not a main priority."

Seeking to place his personal interest and results in perspective, Bob paused, then said, "I'm just an amateur naturalist who has been caught up in this quest. I'm a dreamer. I'd like to think that not everything on the planet has been categorized, that there's still some pocket of natural history and wildness that hasn' t yet been discovered.

"It might be there. It might not be there. It may be a bogus fairy tale I'm tracking, but I think not. Sometimes, I find myself thinking that, in the future, someone will find this thing and say, 'That thing Chance was talking about 25 years ago is really out there.' "

Author's note: Anyone who has experienced an encounter or who may have information on the mid- Atlantic Sasquatch may write to Bob Chance, 3631 Berkley Road, Darlington, MD 21034 or send him an e- mail at [chance- treefarm@aol. com].

'Jefferson Letter Lady'

In Washington, D. C. , on July 2, 1801, 25 years after he had penned the Declaration of Independence, President Thomas Jefferson wrote a letter to the Delaware Baptist Association sharing some of his fundamental views on religious freedom.

For 201 years, this significant document was lost.

In northern Maryland, on March 24, 2002, Joanna Alford, an Historic Elk Landing Foundation volunteer, was in her home carefully sorting through an old cardboard box. It overflowed with the "stuff" most people throw away—old newspapers, bills, personal letters and scraps of papers and trash.

"I picked up a legal size envelope and there were papers folded together, like in thirds," Alford recalled. "And I thought, 'This looks old,' and it was signed by John Quincy Adams. I thought, 'It can't be.' Then I looked at the next one. It was a letter from the Baptist Association that congratulated President Thomas Jefferson on his election to the presidency. And then I looked at the next one, and it was the reply, signed 'Thomas Jefferson!' And I said, 'My God!' "

In the weeks that followed, media representatives, archivists and manuscript experts contacted Alford and members of the fledgling non-profit group. Some didn't know much about Elkton, other than its reputation as the capital of quickie marriages in the 1930s, but that has since changed.

According to Mike Dixon, Cecil County historian and president of the Historic Elk Landing Foundation, the Jefferson letter's discovery has been a shot in the arm for his three-year-old organization. Among those interested was Chris Coover, senior specialist in manuscripts and Americana of Christie's Auction House of New York City. He visited the Maryland site, authenticated the letter and appraised it at more than $700,000.

"Perhaps the real surprise is how the letter survived," Mike said, explaining that "This is a property that has suffered badly through the passage of time."

The story of the how the 42-acre parcel and Hollingsworth plantation house, which housed the Jefferson letter for about 150 years, were saved from a developer's wrecking ball and earthmovers begins about four years earlier, with Jeanne Minner, director of planning for the Town of Elkton.

A real estate agent stopped in her office to inquire about the property's development potential.

Mike Dixon, president of Historic Elk Landing Foundation, and Joanna Alford, foundation volunteer, in front of the plantation house

Joanna Alford

Elkton, Maryland

Jeanne was aware of the site and its location at the confluence of the Big Elk and Little Elk creeks. "Because it was unique geographically and had excellent natural features, I often thought it would make nice parkland," she said.

Eventually, the seller sold it to the town of Elkton, which in 1999 leased it to the Historic Elk Landing Foundation.

When he first saw the condition of the property, Mike realized that reaching his goal to make Elk Landing a northern Maryland version of Williamsburg would take considerable time and effort. Significant fundraising would be needed to stabilize the main structure, which he believes is the northernmost plantation house in the country.

Summarizing the site's colorful history, Mike explained that during the War of 1812, a British invasion led by Royal Marines attempted to attack Elkton, but was turned back by local militia at Fort Hollingsworth, located next to the house at Elk Landing. The invaders were led by Admiral George Cockburn, the same officer whose troops later burned the White House. A bit smugly, Mike added, "The force met its match when they tried the same thing here in Elkton. We sent them packing."

In the 1800s, the site was known for trading and shipbuilding. A fire in 1848 destroyed the original home, and the current house—a Greek revival, three-story structure, complete with slave quarters—was rebuilt in the 1850s on the original foundation. The

One rainy day, Joanna Alford was in her dining room, examining the contents of several boxes. When she saw the Jefferson signature, she called out to her husband, Al, who was in a nearby room.

'I said, "Al. I think I found something signed by Thomas Jefferson!" and his reaction was, "Oh yeah. Great. I'm looking at TV. Don't bother me. Whatever."'

She immediately began to plan to move the document to a safer place. 'All I knew is that I had to get this into the hands of someone who knows more about this than I do.'

Jefferson letter arrived at Elk Landing sometime after that date and went unnoticed for more than 100 years.

In the 1900s, descendants of the Hollingsworth family began to sell off some of the property and lease the home to tenants. Some temporary residents were farmers, who worked the property. Others were long-term renters. Throughout these decades, entire rooms of the building were filled with Hollingsworth family possessions.

"The day we walked in the roof leaked," Mike said, recalling his first visit to the building. "On rainy days water flowed through the house, the porch was ready to fall on your head and the walls of the old stone house could have caved in with a big puff of wind. One of the former tenants said he would go up in the attic, push the old boxes around and mop up rainwater that was sloshing around on the floor."

Jeanne also shared her impressions of the home. "It was filled with materials and boxes. These people were packrats. We came across slave papers and old newspapers. There were ledger books from ships. We actually had real history in our hands. It's amazing that it was sitting there for so long, with so many people going in and out, and that it survived even getting chewed up with all the snakes and insects and mice."

"There were three rooms filled to overflowing with books and material culture, what non-historians would call clutter," Mike said. "It was unorganized. But since the Hollingsworth family was very wealthy and had seen the passage of armies and noted travelers, I

knew we had some of the finest colonial era documents. It was just a matter of going through it all. "

Several volunteers, including Joanna, a retired Maryland social services administrator, agreed to sift through the building's papers. One rainy day, Joanna was in her dining room, examining the contents of several boxes. When she saw the Jefferson signature, she called out to her husband, Al, who was in a nearby room.

"I said, 'Al. I think I found something signed by Thomas Jefferson!' and his reaction was, 'Oh yeah. Great. I'm looking at TV. Don't bother me. Whatever.' "

She immediately sent an e-mail message to other members of the foundation and began to plan to move the document to a safer place. "All I knew is that I had to get this into the hands of someone who knows more about this than I do. "

Mike admitted that when he received Joanna's e-mail he wasn't particularly excited. "People approach me weekly with what they think are valuable documents, including old telephone books and Depression-era newspapers. I thought this was just another routine artifact. "

About two weeks later, when Dwayne Pickett, an archeologist working at Elk Landing, said there might be something to the document, Mike went to examine the letter and was transformed from a skeptic into a believer.

In the following excerpt from the 1801, letter, Jefferson wrote:

I join you, fellow citizens, in rendering the tribute of thankfulness to the Almighty ruler, who, in the order of providence, hath willed that the human mind shall be free in this portion of the globe. That society shall here know that the limit of its rightful power is the enforcement of social conduct; while the right to question the religious principles producing that conduct is beyond their cognizance.

I rejoice too with you in the happy consequences of our revolution, namely our separation from the bloody horrors which are depopulating the other quarters of the earth, the establishment of liberty, equality of social rights, exclusion of unequal privileges civil & religious, & the usurping domination of one sect over another.

"When I looked at the document, " he said, "it was obvious the paper was centuries old, the writing style was distinctive and the signature captured my attention. "

Activity picked up dramatically after a June press conference when manuscript expert Coover described the letter as "a significant find, " and added, "As Jefferson letters go, this is one of the finest I've ever seen. "

Commenting later on the letter, Chris said his appreciation for the letter transcends dollars and cents.

"The content of the Elk Landing letter, " Chris said, "is extremely significant, touching on issues of religious faith, the guarantees of religious freedom in our Constitution and, by clear implication, the importance of maintaining a strict separation between Church and State. Whether you agree or disagree with his interpretation, anyone with a sense of who Jefferson was and his influence over this nation would find this letter compelling and thought-provoking. The issues it addresses are absolutely central to Jefferson's personal philosophy and to his view of the nature of our Constitution and especially, our Bill of Rights. "

Having handled hundreds of presidential letters, Chris said he was not particularly surprised that the document survived unnoticed for so long.

"Letters are compact, " he said, "and tend to get

put in files or bundled up and forgotten. Paper is one of the most durable natural materials, and so, if there are no fires or floods, letters often survive in excellent condition. I have no doubt that there are many important historical letters sitting in boxes or drawers in attics, basements and offices.

"It is sad to say," Chris added, "that historic letters and documents are in more danger from human neglect and indifference than they are from fires, floods and other threats. Old files are often just sent to the dump or recycled and we'll never know what they might have contained. People are too lazy to search very thoroughly, and don't realize the potential value—historical and monetary—that might be there. Fortunately, the volunteers at the Elk Landing Foundation were systematic and careful and the rediscovery of this important letter is their just reward."

"The publicity associated with the discovery," Mike said, "was a windfall. It's something a small nonprofit couldn't buy. We couldn't stop it. It was a like a steamroller coming at us . . . . We've been on radio and television. The Associated Press put our story out on the wire. Historic organizations dealing with religious freedom and Thomas Jefferson, as well as nationally recognized scholars, have been in touch with us."

Mike explained that the only connection between the document and the historic Elk Landing property seems to be the marriage between a Hollingsworth descendant and a gentleman from a prominent Delaware family. That union, which probably occurred well over a century ago, apparently caused the letter to be transported to the Elkton site. "There probably is no way we will ever be able to determine his name or the exact circumstances of how or when the letter arrived here," Mike said.

The foundation board decided it will eventually sell the document and use the funds to pay for improvements to the structures at Elk Landing. However, until the auction, the $700,000 document is in a local bank vault, and a copy is displayed during public events.

"The letter has changed things for us," Mike said. "We don't usually get calls from national scholars," he added. "To a person, the board is very excited. Foundation volunteers are continuing to sift through boxes, and," Mike said with a laugh, "rumor has it that the productivity rate of reviewing documents has picked up considerably."

Joanna also found a paper signed by President John Quincy Adams. But, Mike said, it was simply a request for a newspaper advertisement that a clerk had prepared and bears the president's signature. Its value is in the $5,000 range.

"It's interesting," the Elkton historian added, "before all this happened, I would have thought that was a significant find. Now, it pales in comparison to the Jefferson letter."

As for Joanna, she said she and her husband have developed a newfound interest in the life and works of Thomas Jefferson.

"I think this has all been great," Al Alford said. "The next time my wife says she's got something, I'll listen. That's for sure."

Visit Historic Elk Landing: The Historic Elk Landing Foundation, located in Elkton, Maryland, is working to establish a living history center that will interpret the upper Chesapeake's role in the Colonial and Federal periods and restore the port and plantation. For details on events, visit the web site at [www.elklanding.org], write to Historic Elk Landing Foundation, PO Box 277, Elkton, MD 21922-0277 or call 410 620-6400.

Author's note: A similar version of this story first appeared in *Chesapeake Life* magazine.

Jay Lutz
Wilmington, Delaware

Master Foul Ball Chaser

It was the end of February 2003, about a week after the 26-inch Snowstorm of the Century had paralyzed the area on the previous President's Day weekend. I was sitting in the basement of Jay Lutz's northern Wilmington, Delaware, home.

Interestingly—with cold rain pouring down outside, forming icy streams of water beside high mounds of freshly piled snow—our conversation focused on baseball, America's greatest pastime, which is played in warmer and much more comfortable weather.

Jay, 62, a self-employed technical writer and consultant, said he was getting excited, counting down the weeks until the first pitch of the season would be thrown at the Wilmington Blue Rocks' home opener in April.

Jay admitted that he is a quite a unique baseball fan. In fact, the baseball, itself, is the focus of his attention. For while those in the stands cheer each crack of the bat, hoping for a home run, a triple or a game-winning double, Jay prays for a very different result.

Basically, Jay yearns for foul balls, lots of foul balls, as many as the teams can hit. When the small cowhide-covered sphere soars outside of Frawley Stadium, it becomes fair game for Jay and the other foul ball chasers who wait on nearby streets and parking lots.

Pointing toward a colorful display across the room, Jay began talking proudly about the more than 600 foul balls he has collected since 1999, when he started the hobby.

The hardballs are presented on specially made shelves, which stand 7 feet high, built to accommodate 18 rows from top to bottom. Some shelves hold

five balls, others have capacity for seven in each row. The only thing printed on each round treasured prize is the date that it was grabbed, usually seconds after a disappointed batter slammed it out of the park and allowed Jay the opportunity to give chase.

Some balls, Jay pointed out, will have a black stain, indicating where it hit the asphalt surface outside the ballpark.

A former pitcher at the University of Delaware, Jay said, "Baseball is in my blood, and I like being at the park. But I especially like doing this, because the people are nice and I just enjoy it."

In 1999, when he was looking for a new hobby, he headed down to the Wilmington minor league ball field near I-95 and started chasing foul balls. While it

Each of Jay's foul balls bears the date when it was caught.

may seem a little unusual, Jay said it's a natural thing to do. People of all ages, he said, take their gloves to baseball games, sit in their seats and hope to claim an errant ball that might land in the stands.

Jay's only difference is that he does his waiting outside the gates.

"I like chasing the balls," Jay said. "It's the thrill of the chase. You want to get there before someone else does. Anybody would run to get it. You wouldn't let it sit there. A lot of people would do it, if they weren't so proud. One night, I outran a woman who was chasing a ball that was in the grass. She was in her high heels. When I got it, I gave it to her. I just couldn't keep it."

But Jay admitted he is usually not so generous. Whether his competition is an adult or a youngster, Jay does his best to claim his prize.

A prize-winning Masters and Senior Olympics sprinter, Jay said he can still kick up some dust when it becomes necessary.

"I outrun a lot of teenagers," Jay said, smiling. "I ran right past this kid one night. He couldn't believe his eyes. I never lost a chasing race in a flat out sprint."

Claiming 152 fouls in 2001 and 260 balls in 2002 is not simply the result of racing and luck. Jay said he applies a bit of science to make sure he is in the right place at the right time. Armed with a pencil, batter's chart and handheld radio, Jay listens to the game and adjusts his position outside the stadium based on whether the batter is left or right handed.

The game announcer's commentary will alert the Foul Ball Man that a trophy might be heading his way. After the ball hits the asphalt, the chase begins.

"Sometimes," Jay said, "you'll get a line shot, coming right at you, but I'll let it go and run it down after it hits. Those balls can be going around 80 or 90 miles per hour. You don't try to catch it with your bare hands."

Jay's record for foul balls retrieved in one game stands at 9, and he was skunked only during three of last season's games. His average during the 2002 season was 3.8 balls per game. He snagged 8 balls at four games and walked home with 6 balls seven times.

Proudly, Jay shared a chart that breaks down his personal foul ball stats—by number per game and total per season. He also can compare

Jay points to the areas of the stadium that he focuses on during the game.

these numbers with the figures recorded during previous years.

When asked what people think of his unusual hobby, Jay smiled and said the reactions range from "get a life" to "envy."

Most people who work at the games have become friendly with him. Some consider Jay an extra-added attraction to the Blue Rocks' family atmosphere.

Jay makes a serious effort to attend most home games. (In 2002, he made 61 of the 70 regular season contests.) "When I have to go away on a business assignment," Jay said, "when I get back the parking attendants will say, 'They were flying out there last night.' I probably could have gotten 5 or 10 balls if I was there."

I asked Jay if it was difficult to hold on until opening day, particularly in the midst of winter's chill.

"Only a few more weeks," he said, his voice relaying anticipation. "Right now, there's a really empty feeling. I call this the Dark Ages. I know there are about six more weeks until the chasing begins again. And the closer it gets, the more intense the feeling of anticipation gets.

"I even dream about foul balls," Jay said. "I see myself constantly chasing foul balls at games, trying to run as fast as I can. That's what I do in the winter. But, I could do a lot worse. My wife, Judi, she tolerates it—barely. But," Jay admitted, nodding his head, "my hobby sometimes interferes with our social schedule."

Thinking a few years down the road, Jay said he sees a future master foul ball chaser in the family—his 2-year-old grandson, Kosta. "Maybe he'll do it one day," Jay added. "I'll take him with me and show him how to chase them down. But, it's really all about the little boy in all of us. The more balls you get, the more it gets into your blood. Almost all the men would do it, if their wives or girlfriends wouldn't yell at them about it."

CHARLES J. LUTZ, JR.
Master Foul Ball Chaser
61 Weilers Bend
Wilmington, Delaware 19810
(302) 475-9439

Ron Thomas
Wilmington, Delaware

Dealing in Grave Matters

The sign on the door says "MAAR Associates Inc. ," formerly Mid Atlantic Archaeological Research. It was a weekday night in June, 1999, when I visited the two-story, white warehouse building outside Newark to meet with Ron Thomas, company president and a nationally known archaeologist.

The company's expertise is wide ranging—involving archaeological excavations at primitive sites, studies of historic buildings, historical document research, and analysis and appraisal of American Indian collections. But none of these studious areas was the focus of my interest.

I had come to discuss grave digging—big-time, grand-scale crypt excavation. In particular, I wanted to find out what it was like to move more than 3,000 graves from beneath a parking lot in the center of a major U. S. East Coast city.

And Ron Thomas was the man to see.

He came to Delaware in 1965, from Uniontown, Pennsylvania, to become Delaware's first state archaeologist.

He served for 12 years, until 1977, as the First State's first man serving as an official archaeological authority. In that role, Ron was one of the first persons to be notified when Native American artifacts were discovered or when highway excavations uncovered the remains of historic structures or human bones from an earlier era.

With anthropology degrees from Penn State and the University of Arkansas, plus postgraduate work at the University of Pittsburgh and Temple University, Ron has the right education. More importantly, over the years he and his colleagues at MAAR Associates

have developed the correct combination of experience and interest to be sought by companies and governmental agencies throughout the country seeking guidance on everything from complicated multistage digs to basic identification and evaluation of a single object.

"The smallest project would be a one-day survey where you go to a particular area and you don't find anything," Ron said. "The largest is obviously the Wilmington cemetery, by far—in terms of time spent, in terms of crew size and in terms of finances. There are a lot of places where you can go and you don't find anything."

His largest archaeological project started with a phone call in the spring of 1998.

Ron explained that a construction crew discovered what they believed were human bones while excavating a downtown Wilmington parking lot, near 12th and Jefferson streets. The workers were preparing the site for construction of a new surgical building near the Wilmington Hospital.

"They stopped right away and called the authorities," he said. "Then authorities called Dover. The developers learned about us because we had previously excavated another construction site in Wilmington about two years earlier."

That previous dig was in 1996, and it contained 350 burial sites. At that time, it was the largest cemetery find in the state of Delaware.

The newer 1998 site, referred to as the Old Cathedral Cemetery, would yield nearly 10 times as many forgotten graves; and, Ron said, "This new [1998] site we just excavated contained the largest number of graves ever excavated anywhere to date."

In the U. S. ? I wondered.

"In the world," Ron replied. "Oh, yeah! It just kept on growing and growing and growing."

At the time of the discovery, Ron said he and a representative of the state visited the construction site trailer and looked at what had been unearthed.

"He had a box full of bones," Ron said, "and he obviously recognized them because there was a part of a skull there. That's what caused them to get excited."

There also were coffin hardware and handles, plus some caps and screws. Ron recognized the bones as being human, and he immediately dated the coffin hardware as originating during the 19th century.

Interestingly, Ron said, the construction crew actually brought the find to the authorities' attention. Most of the time when a forgotten burial site is discovered, he said, there's a tendency for workers to ignore the finding, mainly because proper investigation, removal and reburial of remains delays the construction schedule.

In this case, Ron said, when the presence of the cemetery was verified, hospital officials hired Ron and his company to remove the remains as quickly as possible and to hire as many assistants as needed.

The affected area occupied an entire city block that was about three acres in size. As he walked the

site where the blacktop had been stripped away, Ron said he also noticed remnants of tombstones and bone mixed in amongst gravel that had been resting below the macadam. The graves were down about two to three feet below the old gravel surface, he said.

"They [the tombstones] were there," he said, commenting on his walk of the area. "See, what it appears they had done [years ago] when they built the parking lot," he added, "they just pushed them all down. They hauled gravel in and covered them up, and they paved over it. Some of them were in their exact positions, except down. Others [tombstones], they had stuck off in a corner. Nobody had ever noticed them."

As the size of the project increased, Ron's archaeological crew grew accordingly.

"At first we hired 30," he said, "because we figured we were dealing with two or three hundred graves. But as things went on and we started to see how large this was, and that it took up the entire three acres, and they were packed tight. I think, at one time, we had as many as 70 people out there."

His crew worked the site from May 1998 through February 1999. Ron said his workers would wait for machines to scrape off the blacktop and the underlying layer of gravel. Then his people would go through the subsurface dirt with a shovel and try to determine what was underneath. If they found human remains, they would place a flag at the site.

"They would scrape off a hundred foot area, and there would be a hundred flags in there." Ron said. "So we kept hiring more and more people, and we'd do it by sections."

The grave shafts ranged from two to six feet below the current ground surface.

Dozens of archaeologists worked for months on the downtown dig, which resembled a war zone.

Photograph provided by MAAR Associates Inc.

Scraps of wood or metal objects indicated they had hit the top of a coffin. When possible, workers would try to save coffin pieces to preserve the artifacts. Inside the coffin they would find the bones.

"That was one of our problems," Ron said. "In many cases, there were four or five bodies in one grave shaft, stacked. We later found records that indicated that so-and-so was buried in his grandfather's grave. So we'd do it by hand. We have between 10,000 and 12,000 photographs of different stages, many showing the progression of work in each one of these grave shafts."

The bones and skull from each body were dusted and cleaned, then wrapped separately, and the location where they had been found was recorded. Bone specialists and lab experts also were on site to take measurements and conduct studies on the uncovered bones. Field notes, bones and artifacts were placed in boxes and taken to MAAR Associates' Newark site, where a crew would process and inventory each set of remains. Ron said there were about three or four pages of notes and photographs relating to each burial.

The bones were placed in small coffin-like boxes for permanent reburial that eventually took place at a special memorial site, following a ceremony, at All Saints Cemetery on the Kirkwood Highway outside Newark.

Ron said about 40 to 60 sets of separate remains were placed in a single crypt. When each of the deceased was identified, each's remains—plus any clothing or jewelry—was placed in the crypt with the deceased's name, so its identity would be preserved.

Of the 3,181 remains discovered, only about 110 were able to be identified through the use of tombstones, copper or brass nameplates on the coffins and old cemetery records.

> *'After working on so many burial sites, a few of them [archaeological assistants] told me that they intended to be cremated, because they never wanted someone like them digging them up a few hundred years from now.'*
>
> *—Ron Thomas*

"Archaeologists are like itinerant farm workers," Ron said. "You put out a call, you go on the Internet, and in no time at all word gets around and you get the calls. I remember in one week, 13 people came out of Houston. They were working on a cemetery there, and it was finished and they came to us."

MAAR Associates received other calls from as far away as Washington State and Canada.

Ron said archaeological workers are called "field technicians." Most of them have bachelor's degrees. In some cases, he had workers with Ph.D. degrees helping at the Wilmington site.

"They find it exciting," he said, "since it's a chance to work with human bone."

They go from job to job, living in local motels and, in some cases, out of their cars. They bring computers and plug them in, along with mini refrigerators and microwaves.

"It's like a traveling city," Ron said, "but to them the opportunity is worth putting up with inconveniences because they learn an awful lot.

"We had people there who must have excavated a hundred graves," he said, "and that's one person over the period of time they were there. Somebody finds something, and calls out, 'Hey! Look what I've got!' And everybody rushes over. So you learn a lot. We had people from everywhere, and we have some working with us on other projects, now. We just found another cemetery, down near Bear."

Ron said members of his crew are in this for the training and a genuine love of fieldwork. The hourly wage, he said, is not high enough to entice anyone who is not very interested in archaeology. He said the words "enthusiastic" and "exciting" best describe his workers.

"Finding a pair of false teeth that go back to the year 1823, and learning about it is satisfying," he said. "One of the girls working with us ended up writing a national journal article about celluloid. Celluloid was an early form of plastic. It was clear, and it disintegrates over time. They used it to make finger rings, ladies hair combs, toothbrush handles, things of that sort. So they are not just there to dig. They get enjoyment out of finding things, and they're a great bunch of people."

The dig also attracted the interest of staff from the Smithsonian Institute, who made frequent trips to the site, Ron said. There were so many "visitors" interested in the educational aspects of the dig, that Ron assigned one manager to guide visitors.

"He was very busy," Ron said. "Other archaeologists, doctors from the hospital, nurses would come in. Government people, family members. This was an Irish cemetery, and once the word got out there was a lot of interest. The newspaper came and we gave them a big tour.

"We'd do a section and it looked like a war zone, with all these holes, little craters," Ron said. "Of course, we would do an area, then backfill and move to the next section. The whole thing was never exposed at one time, only about two to three hundred graves were open at one time. That would have been quite a photograph, to have 3,000 graves exposed."

Ron said one of the most interesting finds included two cast iron coffins from the 1860s, probably made in Philadelphia. Until this discovery, there were only about 10 similar artifacts excavated in the U.S. Careful attention was given to their removal, then extensive photographs and samples were taken.

Nearly 60 coffins were in stable enough condition to be removed from the ground in whole pieces. Many of these were individual boards, since most of the coffins were wooden, mail order types. But, Ron added, they were the six-sided, hexagonal style. He said his archaeologists found this discovery fascinating, primarily because the use of this type of box seems to have persisted in the Wilmington site years after similar shaped coffins had gone out of style in other parts of the country.

For the average person who lets professional morticians handle the deceased, and who has never seen a dead body in a setting other than in a church or funeral home, the question persists: What is it like working with the remains of human bodies? Is it eerie? Superstitious? Bothersome?

"I dug my first grave back in 1961," Ron said, "and after you do them they become artifacts more than anything else. We realize they're people. We realize they had spirits and souls, and that they walked around. But they're really just artifacts, they're tangible objects."

Ron added that most of his crew thinks the same way. But he admitted that, at times, he's had work-

One of the coffins discovered during the excavation

Photograph provided by MAAR Associates Inc.

ers who could not continue for long handling human remains, and they had to walk off the job.

After working in the field for 40 years, Ron said, you get used to the job and what it demands.

"You no longer have that awe or that fear," he said. "We've been out at night with headlights on to finish a job."

He's heard the legends about people who have been buried alive and their fingers are worn down to the bone, trying to claw their way out of their coffin. While he's never seen evidence indicating that has occurred, there are enough other strange things to investigate.

When they've opened coffins, Ron said they've found bodies resting on their sides, as opposed to lying on their back—because the corpse has been shifted or rolled while being carried to the cemetery or lowered into the crypt.

If bones are missing, he explained, there's a good possibility that rodents carried them off. At times, skulls have been found at the foot of the coffin—because water sometimes gets into a grave and moves the body parts around.

In this last case, Ron said someone might pick up the skull and assume the subject had been decapitated, but that would not be the case.

"Over the years, you learn what to look for," he said.

In the extensive dig at Wilmington's Old Cathedral Cemetery, he said, there were a number of graves that indicated death by some sort of trauma. These ranged from a sword wound to the skull (possibly from a Civil War battle), to battered bones (possibly from physical abuse) to mangled bones (possibly from gunpowder explosions at nearby powder mills).

"If you take care, and you've worked hundreds of these burials," Ron said, "you notice right away where there's something different. You notice when someone is missing a finger, or missing a leg. In one case, we found an artificial leg in the coffin. We had indications that looked like someone smashed a body on the head with a baseball bat or club. Of course, we also found evidence of disease—rickets, syphilis, tuberculosis. So you get a lot of knowledge about the nature of the people and the period in which they lived."

At the time of the original burials, Ron said, embalming was just coming into practice, as was evidenced by a blue powder, probably arsenic, that they found crystallized, covering the bones of a woman they unearthed in an iron coffin.

The crew found many different sizes, materials and shapes of coffins—from infant to adult, from iron to wood. A few even had a plate glass portion placed underneath a wooden lid, so when the it was raised you could view the deceased's body.

Ron explained these were probably used to allow mourners to pay their respects for a longer period of time.

Photograph provided by MAAR Associates Inc.

Ron Thomas (right) directs a crew carrying the remains of a lead coffin.

One of the major discoveries of the dig, in Ron's mind, was the apparent importance of burials by the people who lived in Wilmington at that time.

"I think these people spent a lot of their wealth on treatment of the burials," he said. "Even though they supposedly were poor Irishmen and poor black workers, they really went all out, just from seeing that they bought the high priced items in the catalogs. We did have stratification in the cemetery, with crypts on one side, and widely placed family plots. And when it went downhill toward 12th Street, you came to the paupers' area and unconsecrated ground.

"Now that's a key thing," he added. "Children, who died at childbirth or before they were baptized, were all buried together. We had about three to four hundred children all in that one area. Sometimes they called them 'Children's Gardens.' In some cases they were put in their family plots, it all depends."

Ron also found flower vases, broken wine bottles and goblets, indicating that people used to go out to the cemetery and hold picnics or small parties near a loved one. Old cartridges indicated a military firing squad probably performed a ceremony over the grave.

"We had clergy," Ron said. "There were four of five nuns out there. We had a lot of religious objects —crosses, rosaries, medals, medallions—found in the coffins.

"We found several personal items. One fellow had several scissors in the coffin with him. We figured he was a barber. It was just an interpretation."

Ron has been on nearly 400 digs, and 20 sites were strictly cemeteries, ranging from one grave to the largest—in Wilmington, with more than 3,100 burials. Many were Indian cemeteries, and, he said, there are more cemeteries yet to be unearthed.

But many never will be. It mainly depends on whether development or construction will lead to their discovery.

He said if you look at old city maps, and then visit the sites, it's not unusual to find a parking lot or buildings atop an original burial site. In New Jersey, he said, a landfill now covers an area that once served as a pauper's gravesite. Experts estimate that at that site as many as 10,000 burials are, for the time being, resting in peace.

Ron admitted that his line of work would not appeal to everyone. But he loves the job, and, in particular, he enjoys being in the hunt.

"I like always finding something new," he said, "something that somebody hasn't seen for years. The idea of picking up this object and thinking, 'My God! No one's touched this object for years.' I think it's the idea of discovery. And there's a lot of mystery to it. I think sometimes it's like being a detective, trying to figure out what something is."

As the interview ended, Ron said he wanted to share an interesting comment that he'd been told by more than one of this field assistants.

"After working on so many burial sites," he recalled, "a few of them told me that they intended to be cremated, because they never wanted someone like them digging them up a few hundred years from now."

Author's note: To contact Ron Thomas, call MAAR Associates at (302) 996-0713, or send an e-mail note to [maarassoc@aol.com].

Conversation with Cap'n Jim

Over the years Jim Harris has noticed that a lot of people are envious of his job, and quite a few claim they would love to do what he does—pilot boats for a living.

The 55-year-old sailor spends about half of his year in Delaware City, an historic fishing village and also a major oil refinery port on the Delaware River. But Cap'n Jim's work has nothing to do with oil tankers and barges. His spring and summertime duties focus on piloting the *Delafort*, a 55-foot, 88-passenger, twin-engine ferry operated by the Delaware River and Bay Authority. The vessel's primary duty is to deliver visitors to Fort Delaware—a Union Civil War fort and one-time camp for Confederate prisoners—located on Pea Patch Island in the middle of the river.

We sat in a corner table in the saloon section of the Old Canal Inn, overlooking the river, late on a cool summer evening. The Cap'n had just returned with a full boatload of Fort Delaware Ghost Tour visitors, and Delaware City was ready to roll up the sidewalks and go to sleep.

Cap'n' Jim had the look of a modern day seaman, with the mustache and baseball cap and crows

feet around the eyes, the result of a lot of seasons of squinting at the sun reflecting off the water.

Smiling, he said the townspeople in D. C. , that's how some locals refer to Delaware City, call him "Cap. " At the Fort Delaware State Park, they call him "Cap'n Jim" and his best friends just call him "Harris. " But to long-time companions, old schoolmates and first-time acquaintances, his name's not the attraction, his lifestyle is.

For more than 30 years, since he was 20, the water has played a significant role in Cap'n Jim's life. He started out working as a deckhand on a 65-foot sailboat, to learn the trade from the bottom up, heading out of Miami and cruising to the Bahamas.

"I learned a lot, accumulated sea time, took the tests and eventually got my captain's license, " he said.

The *Delafort* job caught his attention. Since 1993, he's been taking visitors—including historians, school groups, tourists and locals—across the Delaware River to both the island fort and over to the dock at Fort Mott in New Jersey.

"I do this about six months a year, " Cap'n Jim explained. "I enjoy the kids that come on the school groups and I meet a lot of nice people. By the time

Jim Harris

Delaware City, Delaware

the fall arrives, I'm ready to take time off in the winter or work some tugs. Then, I'm ready to come back in the spring."

People have asked him if he gets bored navigating the same river crossing, hour after hour and day after day.

Cap'n Jim smiled and shook his head. "The wheel house of the *Delafort* is my office!" he said, then added that the whole area is his extended operations center—his boat, the town, the park, the river. "I tell people, 'In your office you've got pictures of birds. Here, I've got the real thing!'"

But, he added, working the water is never routine.

Watching out for crab traps, being aware of the weather, current and tides, and keeping alert for passing river traffic are constant duties associated with piloting the ferry.

Cap'n Jim said he's never concerned about the professionals who pilot the big tankers or other full-time fishermen or watermen.

"The weekenders scare me," he said. "I worry about the guy in the 20-foot boat, who has not taken a safe boating class, has no idea of what he's doing and puts the key in it and goes."

Describing himself as "like a fish," he estimates that he spends about 90 percent of his time on the water. That includes 12-hour days preparing and piloting the ferry and several hours sleeping on his 35-foot sailboat that he calls his "water condo."

Meeting interesting people is a bonus of the job, he said, and sometime he runs into someone he's known, or went to school with or took across the river before.

The ferry also provides cruises along the Delaware River and through a portion of the nearby Chesapeake and Delaware Canal.

"I enjoy the night time," Cap'n Jim said. "It's more serene. I guess I'm a night person. I like to look at the moon, stars, various lights. At night, on the river, the lights make Motiva [refinery] look like

a city. It's also not difficult to navigate at night."

In three decades in the business, he's experienced scores of humorous, interesting and crazy stories. After a few moments of reflection, he smiled and shared an incident that happened on the *Delafort*, soon after he had taken the job.

"It was over at Pea Patch, early on," he said, smiling at the memory. "I was looking at the chart for fishing spots, and the passengers had boarded the boat. There was a man with two small sons on the top level, and I was in the wheelhouse, directly in front of them, and they could see me.

"I was taking some extra time looking at the chart, not realizing they were there. I finally rolled it up and looked down at the deck hand, and the man points toward Delaware City [which can be seen from the island], and shouts, 'It's over there Cap!'"

He and other pilots are aware that those who have more traditional jobs are fascinated with ship captains and people who work the water.

"There's a romance or mystique associated with it," Cap'n Jim said. "It may be because of the authority, or that the job doesn't fit the mold, but it's certainly there."

How often does he hear the phrase, "I want a job like yours"?

"I hear it all the time," he replied, smiling. "They say, 'I want to be a sea captain,' and 'How can I do that?' When they tell me, 'I want to do what you do,' I say, 'You have to figure out what will make you happy.'

"Many people don't know what they want to do careerwise. I'm amazed that some people tell me what they want to do is hit the lottery. But when you ask them what they want to do with their life, they don't know. How can you move on without goals and aspirations? I feel privileged that I'm doing what I enjoy doing, and I imagine a very small percentage of people can say that."

Dale Fetzer

Wilmington, Delaware

Living in the Past

There are certain pressure-filled days when we're ready to snap and earnestly wish we were able to be transported magically somewhere far away. Preferably, we would like to end up in a simpler time when life was less hectic and had fewer complications, in an age when technology didn't rule and change at today's rapid pace. Then, just before we return our thoughts back to reality, we wonder, for a brief moment, if there really was such an era—a time when people enjoyed life rather than simply existed from one rat race day to the next.

For several years, Dale Fetzer had a job that enabled him to inhabit—for several hours each day—life during the 1860s, at the height of our country's Civil War.

As lead interpreter at Fort Delaware, located on Pea Patch Island about a mile from the water village of Delaware City, Dale relived history much of his working life.

Standing well over six feet tall, he's an impressive man in stature and bearing. His voice—whether he's in the role of a courteous Confederate gentleman officer or a Union commander—speaks with the authority and authenticity of the characters he has selected to become.

And become them he did.

Within in the thick granite walls of an aging island fortress, Dale dressed in a dark blue Union officer's uniform and lured his audiences into the past. And for five years, from 1997 through 2001, I had the pleasure of working with him each summer and fall, as we co-conducted the popular evening Ghost/History Lantern Tours.

Dale explained that his fascination with the Civil War started about 40 years ago, while he was a youngster growing up near Annville and Hershey, Pennsylvania, not far from Gettysburg.

"God made me do it," he said, while riding the ferry *Delafort* across the Delaware River to Pea Patch Island. "I've been enamored with the Civil War since my earliest memory. The first book I ever recall reading was the biography of Gen. George Armstrong Custer. It's my life."

After studying history in college, he said he existed as a social worker for about nine years and then served a stint in the corporate world. Eventually, he happened to fall into Civil War reenacting and found it to be something he enjoyed. He opened a historical consulting business in 1987.

The rest is . . . history.

He found himself working as an historical consultant and extra on the sets of such well known motion pictures as *Gettysburg, Andersonville, Glory, Lincoln, Ironclads* and *Last of the Mohicans*, to name a few.

His entry into movie production was the result of years of personal interest, serious study and on-the-scene experience.

"There are a lot of reenactors who freelance as experts," Dale said. "I have a background in theater, history and visual arts, and I have a clear and comprehensive understanding of military orders, engagements and maneuvers. I can provide an understanding of the detailed life of a soldier in both the Union and Confederate armies."

Dale said he learned quickly that something has to give when history meets Hollywood. How much of pure history is preserved and what portion is sacrificed on the altar of entertainment is an ongoing struggle. But, he said, such battles are not limited to the big screen. Difficult decisions have to be made every day at living history programs and presentations in parks and historical sites throughout the country.

Smiling as he recalled his experiences on the movie sets, he explained that the relationship

between the movie director and the historical consultant is very important and, at times, delicate. Dale spent a year in Georgia on the set of *Andersonville* and was constantly called upon for input.

"*Andersonville* was most enjoyable," he said. "There was total, complete understanding, and I had wonderful rapport with the director John Frankenheimer."

Dale said that Frankenheimer was noted for firing people on a whim. Therefore, the director was feared by most of the staff and stars. Recalling a humorous incident, Dale said on one occasion, Frankenheimer stopped the filming to examine a sheet of parchment that an actor was using.

"He picked up the writing paper," Dale recalled, "and started asking questions like, 'Is this is authentic paper? How do I know? How can I be sure?' And everyone was waiting and didn't know what to say or

The fort entrance is reached by crossing the stone walkway that stretches across the moat.

do. So finally I said, 'John. You know it because you're paying me a lot of money to know that it's authentic paper.'"

Dale said the entire set was speechless, waiting for the historian to be sent packing. Instead, Frankenheimer laughed and continued along with the shoot.

"When you work on a film," Dale said, "you're involved several months before shooting begins, doing research, visiting sites. With *Andersonville*, I was in Georgia two months before the crew arrived, and I was involved through the final editing process."

While the money can be very good, Dale said, conducting research, being away from home, working constantly and becoming involved in internal studio squabbles make film consulting a taxing field. As he grew older, Dale said he sought a position that would allow him to show off his talents and also push him to continue his research.

For several years, Fort Delaware was the answer.

"I'm doing exactly what I want to do," Dale said, referring to his living history performances, historical studies and preservation work, grant writing and community service. Dale said he is constantly amazed by what he discovers in fort documents that show the site's important role in the history of both the region and country. Sharing what he has learned, he also is the author of *Unlikely Allies*, a best-selling historical reference work about Fort Delaware, which was published by Stackpole Press,

While facts about the fort can be transferred onto reports and placed in printed materials, it's the information about the people who lived, worked and were imprisoned and died at Fort Delaware that Dale uses to make his characters come alive. His portrayal of Fort Commander Gen. Albin Schoepf has caused audiences to applaud and weep.

"I make him live," Dale said of the long deceased Civil War fort commander. "I try to incorporate everything I've read and studied about the man into my presentation. I do a program on the death of his daughter and I cry tears, as if Gen. Schoepf was experiencing the anguish himself. Today, more than 130 years later, I am his voice."

But Dale is more than an actor, more than an historian.

"I'm a teacher," he said. "I teach every day. This fort is my special classroom. We encourage questions. The lessons are learned in a different way, by experiencing the past. We're not only interested in dates and facts. I want the visitors who come here to know why. I want them to know what the people here thought, to see what they saw, to feel what they felt.

"We're telling a complex story that very few Americans are aware of," he added. "We're sharing what happened in the nation we live in. We're giving voice to those who no longer have a voice. Fort Delaware is owned by the people of the state of Delaware. We have the opportunity to tell this fascinating story—about government and tradition and history—in a very different and interesting way."

Dale and the other fort interpreters meet thousands of people each year, and an equal number of incidents occur that provide the performers and employees with a wealth of memories.

To Dale, one special moment stands out.

"I finished performing the story of the death of Gen. Schoepf's daughter. It was toward the end of the season, in 1998, and a man came up to me with tears in his eyes. He said, 'That was wonderful. My name is Josef Holt Pease, from Hockessin, and I am the great, great, great grandson of Albin Schoepf.' He was thrilled," Dale added, proudly, "because I made his ancestor human, and that I brought him to life. I tell you, I felt great. You can't ask for more than that."

Author's note: In 2002, Dale Fetzer changed careers and left Fort Delaware. Some visitors who had toured the Civil War site during the days when he worked there recall Dale's impressive performances.

Currently, he is working as the Apple Computer commercial sales representative at CompUSA and as an authorized Apple education agent. The continuing story of Albin Schoepf will result in a full biography, scheduled for publication in 2004. Dale also is involved with the Delaware Humanities Forum and continues to present performances of Gen. Schoepf. To contact Dale, call 610-357-8367 or send an e-mail to [fetwick1@mac.com].

Fort Delaware State Park: The Civil War fort continues to host a wide variety of living history programs as well as its popular Ghost History Tours, which are offered on certain Friday evenings in the summer and fall. For information and schedules, call the fort office at (302) 834-7941.

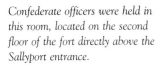

Confederate officers were held in this room, located on the second floor of the fort directly above the Sallyport entrance.

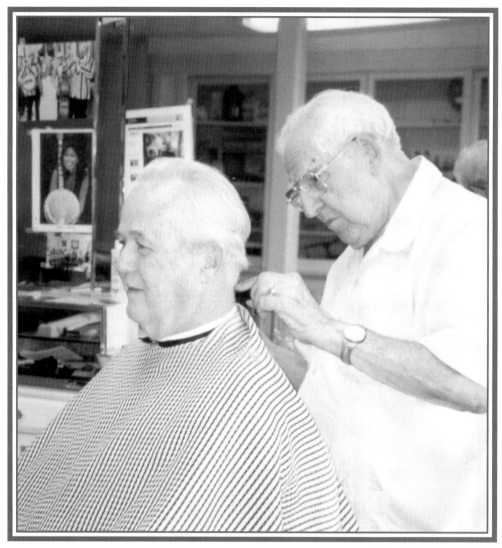

Tony gives regular customer Ray Blankenship a cut.

Tony Trotta

Elkton, Maryland

Tony the Barber

If you want to get the true sense of a town, its present and its past, pay a visit to a real, old-fashioned barber shop. In the case of Elkton, Maryland, there have been a lot of changes since the mid-1930s, and Tony Trotta, 90, has seen them all.

From his vantage point beside a well-worn, red-and-white barber chair at 118 West Main St., he's witnessed the good times and bad, changing customs and on-again, off-again clothing styles.

Tony's seen politicians come and go, consultants and planners offer suggestions about urban renewal, and businesses on either side of his small establishment set up shop and take down the shingle.

Listening to Tony early on a fall morning as he cut the hair of a steady procession of regulars, one wondered if high times would ever return to downtown Elkton. Whatever the result, it would take some doing to match the busiest times Tony had seen in his 66 years working at the same location.

"Main Street has changed," he said. "Back during the war, we had a lot of activity—soldiers from Aberdeen, sailors from Bainbridge. You had to walk in the street it was so crowded on Saturday and Friday nights. Then Triumph [munitions factory] had 8,000 girls working over there."

He started cutting hair in 1936 for his father-in-law, the late Anthony Williams, who owned the Main Street business and had a view through the very same window. Tony was 23 years old at the time. He was born in Wilmington, Delaware, in 1913, worked a while in a leather factory and also laid some blacktop.

"I decided I wanted to do something easier," he said, pausing from his scissors work on decade-long regular Arthur Jones of Elkton.

"He gives a good cut!" Arthur said, offering an unsolicited testimonial about his barber.

"I like this job," Tony continued, smiling. "I got customers I can talk to. I got musicians who come in and play." Tony paused to explain that he can dust a banjo and guitar fairly well, and at times fellow musicians will stop in and break out their instruments.

"When I started in the business, a haircut cost 25 cents," Tony said. "Now it's six dollars. I know most of my customers by name. My busiest day used to be Friday and Saturday, but not any more."

Part of the shift from weekend business, the barber said, might be that not many Main Street stores are open on Saturday. "I think I'm one of the oldest businesses still operating. Stanley's [Newsstand] was the oldest, but they since closed up. I think the trouble with Elkton is the shops are closed up too many days a week.

"But I think the town is picking up. There's a new restaurant on the corner. I go there and eat. They got pizzas. It's a nice place."

As the interview continued, Ray Blankenship—who described himself as a 15-year, satisfied patron from Elkton—settled into the soft leather throne recently vacated by customer Jones.

"I like my barber," Ray said, nodding toward the white-haired man holding a straight razor. "I can sit here and talk. We see how each other are getting along. We go to the same back doctor, too."

That comment caused Tony to inquire about the condition of Ray's lower discs, and for a brief while the men talked about health in general. As Tony resumed combing and cutting, Ray settled into a relaxed state, confident that his barber would provide a quality cut.

Those familiar with barber shop etiquette and custom know that conversations in the hallowed room, mainly populated by males and designated by a swirling red-white-and-blue pole, tend to jump around a bit. The talks also are characterized by abrupt stops and starts, and the focus of the ever-flowing dialogue tends to drift off in several directions at once.

Newcomers passing through the tonsorial parlor's door on any given day and moment may find themselves updated on a discussion that had just concluded or they may casually toss an entirely new topic into the mix. This sometimes causes repetition, misunderstanding and, most often, side comments delivered from waiting patrons.

Talk shifted in the direction of Elkton's marriage heyday, the glory years when the town was on the national map. Thanks to a law that did not require a waiting period to get hitched, Elkton was known as the romance capital of the world. Naturally, business at that time was not only brisk, it was downright wild.

Tony and others in the room nodded when he talked of cab drivers chasing down potential couples, busy chapels along the city's streets and marrying ministers, with names like Rev. Lambert, Sturgell and Hopkins, who advertised their services. One sensed Tony could almost see the hectic street traffic, the commerce generated from visitors filling up hotels, restaurants and jewelry stores, and the trains and busses dropping off lovers who couldn't wait to tie the knot and proclaim "I do!"

"I wish they had it back," Tony said. "The busses, trains. They brought couples into town. The cab drivers would take them to the minister and then get their cut. The guy on the train, he got a cut, too. If a couple was walking down the street, they would stop them and ask if they were looking for a minister . . . . It was really nice. Everybody made money. They'd buy rings. The restaurants would be busy."

But times change, and life goes on. And barbering, too, is not what it used to be.

Pointing to the two empty barber chairs facing the large wall mirror, Tony said, "I used to have three barbers. The place was filled with people waiting. After women started with hair styling, the wives started taking their children to the other place. I think some men started going there with their wives, which is all right. I don't care.

"We're not as busy as we used to be. Beauty shops have taken over a lot of men's hair cutting. Beauticians. I don't know why these fellas pay $15 to $20 for a haircut. But they do a good job."

Tony Trotta and Marshall Purner pose for a picture.

Ray turned his head and added his opinion. "Once you get used to a barber, you're comfortable. I don't ever have to tell Tony my cut. He knows how I like my hair."

Obviously appreciating the compliment, Tony smiled and said, "I stick to old ordinary haircuts. The others do a lot of styling. I don't. This is a barbershop."

Marshall Purner, a retired Elkton police officer, had slipped in during the conversation. The North East resident said he had been using Tony's services for 37 years.

"He's reliable and professional," said Marshall, another regular and one known to provide musical entertainment on occasion.

Tony, who still works six days a week at the age of 90 has strong opinions about retiring.

"That's why I keep working," he said. "I don't want to retire!"

"Don't let him kid you," Marshall shouted from his chair across the room. "He likes the money! He likes to pay cash for those big Buicks!"

Stopping again, and walking a few steps from his white-draped client sitting in the chair, Tony said, "A lot of people say to me they think I'm only 60 years old. That makes me feel young. And my advice is this, everybody I talk to says, 'When I get to be 62, I'm gonna get my Social Security. I'm going to retire.'

> *'This barbershop is in a vacuum in time. Once it goes, it will never be the same.'*
>
> —*Marshall Purner*

"I think that's foolish. That's a good way to sit down and die. So if you don't like a job, you got to find something else until you do and then do that."

"And don't play the horses!" Marshall shouted.

Tony admitted that barbering is a dying profession. The hours are too long, there's no retirement plan and people need health benefits in today's world.

"But it's a clean job," he said, smiling. "And," pointing his comb at Marshall, Tony added, "I got a retired cop in the corner who comes in and sweeps the floor. But I like the customers. We joke and kid. A lot of people like to come in because we laugh and kid around. I even get people that don't get their hair cut who come in and talk."

For a moment the room became silent. It was an awkward few seconds. Thoughtful, as if those present wanted to capture the moment, save it in a jar.

Then Marshall, every bit the jokester, walked across the room, looked at Tony, then glanced at the others in the familiar hangout, and said, "This barbershop is in a vacuum in time. Once it goes, it will never be the same."

Author's note: A similar version of this story originally appeared in *The Cecil Whig.*

Jean and Bob Patterson, at a traveling replica of 'The Wall,' the Vietnam Veterans Memorial, when it visited Elkton, Maryland

Bob and Jean Patterson

Elkton, Maryland

Mobilizing for the POW/MIA Postage Stamp

There's a flag pole in the front yard of a ranch house in the development of Meadowview, outside Elkton, Maryland. Directly below the Stars and Stripes is the distinctive black-and-white POW/MIA flag, bearing the silhouette of an American prisoner of war.

Bob Patterson—now 55 and an engineering technician at the Perry Point Veterans Administration Medical Center in nearby Perryville—recalled how he got involved in a life-changing project, 11 years ago.

While Bob was hanging out with a few close friends, someone mentioned that rock 'n' roll legend Elvis Presley was to be featured on a U. S. postage stamp. Bob remembered that he said it would be more appropriate that a stamp be issued to honor those U. S. service personnel who were prisoners of war (POWs) and missing in action (MIA).

Thinking back on that casual conversation, Bob said he never would have imagined that it would turn into a nationwide, grassroots campaign that generated almost 2 million signatures of support for a stamp honoring POWs and MIAs. But the four years of hard work had its intended result—the creation of the POW-MIA stamp.

But the story of the stamp really begins before that day when Bob and some friends were shooting the breeze. It started several decades ago and a half a world away from his Maryland home, in South Vietnam.

Bob served his country as an infantryman in the U. S. Army, 1st Air Cavalry Division in Vietnam from 1967-68. A member of Veterans of Foreign Wars, Post #6027, in North East, Maryland, he and his wife, Jean, have three children.

As a veteran, Bob said he has a few friends who are still missing in action.

"I believe they fought for their country," he said, "and they need to be brought home, so their families can finally close the chapter. And we should let the rest of the public know we have people still missing, that are unaccounted for, from all the wars."

Those feelings are shared by millions of Americans. What makes Bob different is that he went far beyond talking about how he felt. He and Jean decided that a postage stamp honoring POWs and MIAs was important, and they decided to make it happen.

"We drafted a petition and started going to different events and passed them out," he said, "and we just asked people to sign them. And nobody ever said no. No one ever turned us down. They all said it's about time somebody did something, that those missing in action need to be recognized."

Since they are both Harley-riding motorcycle enthusiasts, the Pattersons decided to use their weekend riding hobby as a way to spread the word about their grassroots stamp effort. They went to cycle rallies in Maryland, Delaware, New Jersey and Pennsylvania—always with copies of their petition in hand. Bob said they also rode to national and regional rallies with the Vietnam Vets Motorcycle Club and handed petitions to delegates from each state.

Eventually their cause rolled across the country with the help of an unknown number of sympathetic two-wheeler drivers.

"We attended the Delaware V. F. W. state convention. We'd go to Washington, to The Wall, and pass them out there," he said. "Eventually, people were taking them and making copies on their own, and sending them in to us from all over the country. They also were sending them directly to the postmaster general and the U. S. Postal Service. "

Soon the mail carrier was delivering stacks of mail to the Patterson home.

"We got letters from all over the country," Jean said. "They were from kids in sixth grade classes and ex-POWs, from family members of MIAs. Everybody. I even got some from service people in Bosnia, Sarejevo, Germany, Australia and England. "

"We'd get 10 envelopes a day, with 20 to 25 petitions in them. " Bob said. "When it started we got big envelopes with 500 to 600 signatures. In Mississippi, a veteran's newspaper printed a copy of the petition and school kids took a copy of it and got signatures. "

"We got petitions from prisoners in prisons," said Jean, smiling. "I replied to them from our post office box. "

Laughing, Bob added, "When we got the petition printed in *Playboy* magazine, all hell broke loose. "

Realizing that the effort was getting a larger response than they had anticipated, Bob got a post office box at Perry Point, where he still works.

"I would get stacks of so many letters that they wouldn't fit in the box," he recalled. "The postmistress would say, 'I got some more for you. '

"I'd say we got more than 2 million signatures," Bob said. "When I went to Washington in 1994 and spoke to Mr. Tolbert, who was manager of Stamp Management of the U. S. Postal Service Headquarters, I took three boxes full. And he said, 'We're getting a lot of them, too. ' "

Sorting, opening and filing, plus organizing the

mail that needed a response, became a second full-time job for both Bob and Jean.

"On an average week," he said, "we'd spend about five to six hours a day. Jean helped me with everything. Between the two of us, we put in at least 50 hours a week. On Saturdays and Sundays, we'd sit at the picnic table in the summer and write letters. It depends on what came in the mail. A lot of people sent two and three page letters, and you had to reply. You just couldn't ignore them. "

Jean agreed, adding, "I spent years writing letters. I replied to thousands and thousands. I had writer's cramp. "

When they first started the project, the Pattersons had no idea that they would become the center of a national emotional hurricane.

"When I first started, I figured we'd get some signatures, and it would go a little ways, and that would be it," Bob said, shaking his head. "But the American public stood behind this 100 percent. There's a time when you work so hard at something, and there's no opening at the end of the tunnel, and things almost get to a stop. Then you would get one letter that would inspire you to keep pushing and pushing and pushing. After I got a newspaper article, about the kids in Water Valley School District in Mississippi, and a letter from them with 804 signatures, I told my wife I have to keep this going. I knew it would happen. "

But more than petitions were included in the mail. Every petition comes back with a little handwriting down the side, or a note attached. Some wrote, "I'm an ex-POW," or "I'm a brother of someone who is missing," or "It's about time. "

"Some of the letters put a lump in your throat," Bob said. "I've gotten personal letters from sons and daughters of people who are missing. It hurts so deep

inside that it was overwhelming. You have to send a personal letter back to than, rather than just add them to the stack. People even send flags. We've gotten five or six POW/MIA flags. We donated them to churches, schools. I sent one to the school in Mississippi. I donated one to the town of Perryville and Havre de Grace. I've got one for Elkton. "

The American commemorative stamp features the words:

"POW & MIA Never Forgotten" on a set of military dogtags (identification tags) set against the background of a waving American flag.

The description page, provided by the U. S. Postal Service states:

". . . the stamp honors those American service personnel still unaccounted for and all veterans captured by hostile forces and terrorists and remembers those who remain missing in action. The stamp draws national attention to the POW & MIA issue and recognizes all who served and suffered as well as those who continue to serve. It symbolizes our long-standing commitment to never forget our citizens and service members lost or captured during time of war or international conflict. "

On Memorial Day, May 29, 1995, the Pattersons attended a formal unveiling ceremony to commemorate the POW/MIA stamp in Washington, D. C. There also was a Second Day Issuance ceremony of the stamp at Perry Point V. A. Center Post Office on May 30, in the Pattersons' honor.

After all these years, one wonders what the Pattersons think when they recall the overwhelming international response to their initial idea.

"I feel real good, " Bob said. "It took a total of seven years, and it's something that needed to be

> *While Bob was hanging out with a few close friends, someone mentioned that rock 'n' roll legend Elvis Presley was to be featured on a U.S. postage stamp. Bob said it would be more appropriate that a stamp be issued to honor those U.S. service personnel who were prisoners of war (POWs) and missing in action (MIAs).*

done. And the American people have shown their true feelings towards veterans. When I found out that we got the stamp, I just started trembling inside. I don't know how to explain it. It's overwhelming. I'm not the only one who worked on this. There were a lot of people across the country. I'd like to thank everybody, to each and every citizen in the United States that supported and helped in obtaining the POW/MIA stamp. "

"To me, " Jean added, "it's still like it all happened yesterday. At the Perry Point Post Office, when I walk in there and talk to Brenda, the postmistress, and see the picture of the ceremony and the flag, it's like it just happened yesterday. "

"But, " added Bob, "I wish that all the men who fought in the wars had returned home, so we wouldn't have to do something like this. "

Author's note: On Sept. 18, 1998, Bob and Jean Patterson visited "The Wall That Heals, " the Traveling Vietnam Veterans Memorial, during its stop in Elkton, Maryland, on a nationwide tour.

Looking at the 246-foot replica of the original monument that stands on the Mall in Washington, D. C. , Bob, who had helped erect the traveling structure, said, "I started out okay. But once it got set up, and I saw the names again, I got an eerie feeling. Like I was in D. C. When they turned the lights on, that was it. It's hard to explain, but it still gives me goosebumps when I see The Wall. "

Photograph by Jerry Rhodes

'Corky' Jones

New Castle, Delaware

Crab Taxidermist

The basement of Corky Jones's New Castle, Delaware, area home is a taxidermist's dream. Lining the walls are all sorts of creatures, representing the diversity of nature and the dexterity of hand and keenness of eye that Corky brings to his craft.

Examples of his handiwork include deer heads, flying squirrels, Canada geese, ducks and odd-looking, devil-ray appearing creatures called angler fish. Then, there is his special creation, the blue-clawed crab.

Corky remembered how he got started in working with what would become one of the most sought after items among his many loyal customers.

"About 20 years ago," Corky said, "a guy that I was working with told me about his dad, who lived in Florida and was doing taxidermy work with shellfish. I just started to follow what that guy was doing."

Today, his preserved specimens of these creatures of the sea makes a casual gift shop browser stop an ask, "Is it real, or isn't it?"

Corky noted that working with crabs is a tricky business, mainly because the shell of the creature is so fragile and the insides deteriorate so quickly.

People bring crabs to Corky in both a fresh or frozen state, including some crabs that have suffocated while being shipped to area restaurants.

"During the off-season, my crabs come from the Gulf of Mexico," he said. "But when crabbing season is in full swing in the Delmarva area, I get them from local sources."

The preservation process begins when Corky places an identification tag on the claw of each of the crabs he is going to work with. Then he submerses them in a five-gallon plastic bucket teaming with a solution of formaldehyde and water. The mixture kills the meat inside the crab and also acts as a disinfectant.

Later, the crabs are taken outdoors, where they are placed on the top of a rack-like table to cure in the open air while the chemical evaporates. When the shells turn brown, they are ready to bring back indoors for painting.

For this task, Corky likes to use a selection of oils that range in color from blue to orange to maroon.

"Some people I know have moved on from oils to acrylics, but I have stayed with the oils," Corky said. "I just like them better."

Brushes of all shapes and sizes—with names like fly-speckers and fans—line the shelves of his basement studio. Once a crab is painted to his satisfaction, the creature gets a coat of urethane to protect its surface and add rigidity to the somewhat brittle skeletal structure of the crab.

Getting just the right color, while maintaining the individuality of each piece, is something that Corky credits to a lot of teachers and friends who have shown him various methods, including Bill Caine, the proprietor of Caine's Wharf in Rock Hall, Maryland.

The result of all this effort is a creation so lifelike, that if a person were to place one of the crabs into an aquarium or pond, an unsuspecting onlooker would expect the creature to scamper off, looking for food or protective cover.

Although Corky doesn't recommend immersing his finished crabs into any kind of liquid solution, he does spend a great deal of time roaming the banks of

the Delaware River, looking for pieces of driftwood on which to mount the finished products.

Corky figures that he sells upwards of 300 crabs each year, and that the demand for his work has grown steadily over the years—mostly from word-of-mouth endorsements from satisfied customers.

His work can be found throughout Delmarva, in places ranging from the New Jersey Wetlands Museum, just outside of Ocean City, to Lestardos' Restaurant, near Hares Corner, New Castle. Maryland locations where Corky's crabs are sold include Lighthouse Gifts, south of Chesapeake City, and Kathy's Corner in North East.

While the blue-clawed crab is his specialty, Corky also does the same thing with other shellfish, most notably with a critter called "spider crab." He has also done lobsters, but the demand is not that great in the Mid-Atlantic region.

"I guess that's because this is crab country," he said. "The crabs are to Delmarva what the lobsters are to folks up in New England."

While the majority of his customers are local, some come from as far away as Connecticut and North Carolina. He has even shipped his blue-clawed beauties out west to Colorado.

The largest denizen of the deep that Corky ever worked on was a seven-foot marlin, caught back in the days before the enactment of federal and state government catch and release laws.

Today, he noted, most of these reproductions are done with fiberglass models, or blanks, which are available from various trade publications and hunting and outdoors magazines.

You can get them for marlin, shark and sailfish, as well as sunfish and mackerel. If it suits your fancy, he said, you can even obtain a fiberglass model of an octopus.

Working with these materials involves trimming the excess moulds of plastic from certain edges, much in the same manner as model builders trim the cars and planes they are about to assemble and paint.

Once a blank fish has been fashioned into the correct shape, it's time to put in the glass eyes and sand the skin to get just the right texture for painting.

"I use the same techniques that I use for the crabs," he said. "At first I didn't like the fiberglass blanks, but now I really enjoy working with them. They have gotten a lot more realistic over the years."

Besides being pleased with the increasingly lifelike skin texture of these fiberglass fish and shellfish, Corky said it's a bit healthier, because no chemicals are needed in preparing the fish for painting.

Corky retired from Occidental Chemical Co. in New Castle about eight years

Photograph by Jerry Rhodes

Crabs waiting for a paint job and a new home.

ago. He recalled that he got started in his present hobby when he was 12 years old in his hometown of Essington, Pennsylvania. It all began when he saw an ad in a hunting magazine and signed up for a correspondence course with the J. W. Ellwood School of Taxidermy in Omaha, Nebraska.

"As a beginner, you work with animals like pheasants, and that sort of thing," he said. "The thing is that these animals have a lot of feathers, and feathers can cover up a lot of the mistakes made by a newcomer."

When he moved to Delaware in the late 1950s, Corky said there were only a few taxidermists in the state. He recalled how one of these guys, the late Bob Beck, helped him to get started in the business. Beck was a wildlife enthusiast who later donated his entire collection of wildlife artifacts in 1976 to the Port Penn Museum.

"In Delaware, you needed a business permit to sell these things, so someone told me to get in touch with this Beck fellow, because he knew everything about what I wanted to do," Corky said. "I called Bob, and he ended up being one of my best friends."

Although working with crabs gives Corky plenty to do during warm weather, it is the hunting season

Photograph by Jerry Rhodes

of late fall and early winter that tends to be his busiest time of the year.

"I do deer heads and ducks," Corky said. "The hardest thing I've ever done was a porcupine. That thing just kept sticking me every time I touched it."

Corky credits his success and enjoyment of his craft to the support of his wife of 50 years, Chris, a lady whom he says puts up with all the things that go with being married to a taxidermist.

"I have been blessed with a very patient wife," he said. "She has put up with people dragging all kinds of animals and fish in her house."

For Corky, having the support of his family and friends, meeting new people and enjoying his hobby all adds up to a very satisfying way of living.

"You meet some real nice people," Corky said. "I have enjoyed it all these years—it's just something that I love to do."

—*Jerry Rhodes*

Author's note: To contact Corky, call (302) 328-6389.

Felix Cartagena

Newark, Delaware

The Bubble Man

The message, "Not a business . . . just a lifestyle," printed at the bottom of Felix Cartagena's business card is more than a clever statement, it's a principle of human behavior that he demonstrates regularly—in a rather unique way.

Known affectionately to his many fans and friends as the "Bubble Man," Felix, 55, is a familiar figure at kite flying competitions and community events up and down the Delmarva Peninsula.

Because of his bubble fame and the visibility his handmade bubble machines command, few realize that Felix also is an accomplished kite-builder. He has won numerous prizes in that field from such nationally recognized organizations as the Smithsonian Institution, where he took top honors in theme competitions at the 1999 and 2000 Smithsonian Kite Festivals.

And while his winning kite design of 1999 is in the hands of the Smithsonian, the Newark, Delaware, resident is best known locally for his "ephemeral sculpture" or bubble-making machines.

"I see bubble making as performance art, but as one step removed," Felix stated in his *Bubble Manifesto*. "It is not the making of the bubbles but the bubbles themselves that are the performance."

An amateur inventor, who works at a company called Tools and More, Felix created his first bubble machine in the early 1980s. He said it grew out of his involvement in various kite-flying events, where the bubbles are used to gauge wind direction and changing air currents.

As in all serious fields of endeavor, there is a skill to bubble making. It starts when Felix pours bubble soap, which he buys by the carload in 100-ounce bottles, into a standard ice cube caddy of the type found in most refrigerators. This vessel, usually about a foot long and eight inches or so in depth, also houses a wheel to which a host of bubble wands are attached.

When power from a 12-volt battery is switched on, the bubble wand spins its way through the soap-filled container, and the bubbles are propelled aloft by a fan mounted on a wooden platform that is secured to a metal pole.

The result is a rainbow of colors and kaleidoscope of spherical designs that attracts hordes of children in a way that would make the Pied Piper envious.

While acknowledging his part as a mini creator in the bubble-making process, Felix believes it is Mother Nature who is ultimately responsible for visual delights that follow.

"The machine and the vagaries of the wind create the art," Felix said. "Every nuance of the wind is captured by the ephemeral film that glimmers and shimmers, making visible the prismatic colors of light."

To give others a chance to experience the joys of his art, Felix has served as professor of bubble-ology at the American Visionary Arts Museum in Baltimore, holding forth with weekend workshops on one of his favorite subjects, "Bubble Gizmo-ology 101: Inventing, Bubbles & Inventing Bubbles."

Casually, the Bubble Man mentioned, "The American Visionary Arts Museum has two of my bubble machines."

To assist him at many of his performances, Felix enlists the help of two of his favorite creations, Hank the Crank Bear and his Bodacious Bubble/Machine, and the Grateful Dead Dancing Bears, which features dancing teddy bears on each side of a bubble machine, churning out bubbles by the gazillions.

These tender tributes to the original tough, rough riding "Teddy" Roosevelt are also a big hit at kite flying festivals, like the one held by the Maryland Kite Society at Ft. McHenry National Park in Baltimore.

Released in flight by a device that causes the bears to parachute from about 100 feet above the crowd, one of his stuffed teddies—Mr. Winston Dashiell Bear—landed slightly off target and plunged into the waters just beyond the park grounds. An alert fellow kite enthusiast rescued the bear, gave it CPR and showed it to the kids, who were much relieved to see that their favorite stuffed animal was none the worse for wear despite missing the intended target area.

It's the squeals of laughter from kids, and sometimes even grown-ups, that make both the bears and the bubbles so much fun to do, Felix said.

92

For the past decade he has been a summertime regular, appearing as an added attraction at the Wednesday Night Concerts at White Clay Creek State Park, just outside Newark, Delaware.

Felix also has performed at other more prominent venues, like the 1997 Smithsonian kite festival, where he used 15 gallons of bubble soap to create a swirling trail of bubbles that delighted the many youngsters in the crowd.

Late summer and early fall, with the often warm, humid days, provide some of the best bubble-making opportunities, Felix said.

"On one of these days last October, I literally flooded the boardwalk in Ocean City, New Jersey, with bubbles," he said, smiling. "A little girl came up to me, and said, 'this is the best day of my life.'"

Often, Felix said, he will get a letter from someone telling how they were having a pretty low day until they saw all those bubbles, and how the rising of those shimmering spheres lifted their spirits.

A unique experience, Felix said, is to make bubbles at night, using a 500-watt quartz halogen flood lamp, with the result that only the bubbles are illuminated against what he describes as "the velvet of the night." Some have exclaimed that the sight is "better than fireworks."

Although some might wonder how a person could find so much delight in such a seemingly simple pastime, Felix said he can't really explain the attraction, and figures it is somewhere out there on an intuitive and mystical plane.

"I just know I like to make bubbles," Felix said. "I like to watch bubbles, and I like watching people watching bubbles. It is unspoken harmony with the universe."

—*Jerry Rhodes*

Author's note: To contact The Bubble Man, send him an e-mail note at [Dbubbleguy@aol.com] or call him at (302) 737-4689.

'I see bubble making as performance art, but as one step removed. It is not the making of the bubbles but the bubbles themselves that is the performance. By creating the apparatus that makes the bubbles, there is no artist per se. The machine and the vagaries of the wind create the art. Every nuance of the wind is captured by the ephemeral film that glimmers and shimmers, making visible the prismatic colors of light. The forms that billow forth are very much subject to one's personal interpretation, much the same as two people looking at a cloud and seeing different things. The addition of music to the performance can influence the mind set of interpretation but certainly is not necessary.'

—*Felix Cartagena*
an excerpt from his work
'The Bubble Manifesto'

The authors, Jim (left) and Ray, holding a brick believed to be from the original home site of the Jersey Devil

Jim McCloy and Ray Miller Jr.

Newark and Wilmington, Delaware

Tracking the Jersey Devil

Think about New Jersey and certain images immediately come to mind. Some are associated with scenes from HBO's hit mobster series *The Sopranos*. Visions of sand dunes along the Jersey Shore, experiences in Atlantic City (Steel Pier days of old and casino junkets of times more recent) certainly are right up at the top. Toss in sleepy memories of stops at roadside stands filled with fresh Jersey tomatoes, or appearances by Bruce Springsteen at the Stone Pony Bar, and you've pretty much covered the coastal state's principal trademarks.

Not quite.

Predating all of the above is the infamous Jersey Devil, a mysterious creature of mythology and history, of folklore and legend, that has captivated residents of the Garden State and beyond for more than 260 years.

Very few states can claim their very own monster, especially one with such a horrid and threatening appearance. Descriptions of the creature's size have ranged from 18 inches to 20 feet. It's said to have the body of a kangaroo, the head of a dog, the face of a horse, the wings of a bat, the feet of a pig and a forked tail. Different reports state that it hops, flies, runs and, of course, breathes fire.

It's no wonder that two young boys, growing up in New Jersey in the 1940s and '50s were aware of and captivated by the legend of the beast.

> 'The stories drive the imagination and the legend. But there's something out there in the Pine Barrens. We've seen the footprints and heard the reports that just can't be explained.'
>
> —Ray Miller Jr.

Ray Miller Jr., 59, now of Wilmington, Delaware, was born and raised in Elizabeth, at the northern end of the state. "I had an uncle that did hunting and fishing in the Pine Barrens," Ray recalled. "He would tell us stories about it, so I was aware of the legend since I was very young."

For James "Jim" F. McCloy, 62, now of Newark, Delaware, his orientation about the creature occurred in Haddonfield, which sits on the fringe of the Devil's stomping grounds. "I heard about the Jersey Devil since I was a kid, ever since I was learning to read. I remember going through Camden and seeing a sign that said, 'Home of the Jersey Devil.' I wondered, 'What's that?' When we would go to the shore, we would pass through the piney woods on the way to Long Beach Island and tell stories about the Jersey Devil. And we heard stories about people who would go camping and hear noises."

In the mid 1970s, the two men met while both were full-time faculty at Wilmington College. Jim was presenting classes in history and Ray was teaching English.

For several years, Jim had been collecting newspaper clippings and articles about the New Jersey legend. After talking with Ray, who also expressed interest in the topic, Jim suggested that they pool their resources and work on a book about the legendary creature.

Over the next two years the writing progressed, resulting in *The Jersey Devil* in 1976, based primarily on library and document research and about one-fourth on personal interviews.

"We would talk to people and they would tell us their stories,' Jim said, "or they would say we should go and talk to so-and-so."

During the field research on that first book, Jim said, people were a little reluctant to share their tales. But, when the two authors were writing the follow-up volume—*Phantom of the Pines: More Tales of The Jersey Devil*, released in 1998—the authors said they found folks were more eager to share their comments, hearsay and anecdotes.

After more than a quarter century of work on the New Jersey creature, Jim and Ray are considered recognized experts on the topic. They have presented hundreds of lectures—in settings ranging from libraries and conference halls to colleges and bookstores. Radio and television interviews are ongoing and peak around the Halloween season. They have appeared in films

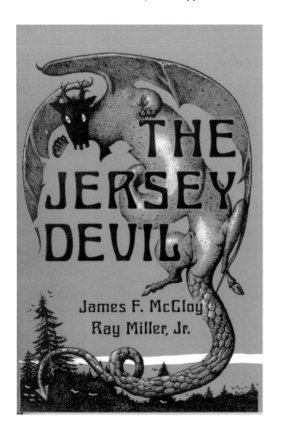

and documentaries about the Jersey Devil that have aired on both cable and network television.

"We've made a lot of trips back and forth to the Pine Barrens," Jim said, recalling the large number of interviews the two of them have conducted.

"But it's been a lot of fun," Ray said, "meeting people, talking with them at a variety of locations. We went to a number of events, including the New Jersey Folk Festival, where we presented talks and also got a number of leads."

So what is the fascination with this Jersey Devil? Why has it commanded enough attention to have its name plastered across the uniforms of a National Hockey League team and become the basis for the Jersey Devil cocktail, which is served in the Smithville Inn?

"You've got an unexplained phenomenon," Ray said, " similar to the Yeti or Loch Ness monster or UFOs. But this one is identified with an unusual place. You've also got active folklore that has been passed from generation to generation. It also shows how monsters fit into the culture of history and the world."

According to Jim, the Devil is unusual because, "It's still active today. There are continued sightings. This is not like the Mothman story that was a one-week wonder. Events and sightings continue to happen, and they feed off each other. The legend goes back to 1735 and it has been nurtured by different groups of people."

One of the areas where the Jersey Devil legend established a firm hoof hold was Philadelphia. Since many of that Pennsylvania city's citizens spend summer vacations along the Jersey Shore, it was inevitable that residents of inner city row houses and Main Line mansions eventually spread tales of the forest creature.

In 1909, the Phantom of the Pines apparently paid a visit to its Philly fans and the creature also terrorized residents of numerous Garden State communities.

"That was the big year for sightings," Jim said. "It came out of the Pine Barrens and raided Philly."

During that week of Jan. 16-24, 1909, he explained, the hysteria associated with Devil reports was very similar to the UFO sightings of today.

According to police documents and newspaper accounts at the time, the monster had been spotted, or its hoof prints discovered, in such New Jersey locales as Burlington, Camden, Woodbury, Westville, Mount Holly, Riverside, Collingswood, Haddonfield, Pemberton, Haddon Heights, Trenton, Gloucester City and more. Across the Delaware River, it was sighted in Philadelphia, Bristol and Liperville in Pennsylvania. There also were reports in Wilmington, Delaware, and in Maryland, California and Canada.

In *The Jersey Devil*, the authors note that the descriptions of the flying/hopping/running visitor were quite colorful. Witnesses employed such terms as "jabberwocky," "kangaroo horse," "flying death," "kingowing," "woozlebug," "flying horse," "flying hoof" and "prehistoric lizard."

But the two Devil experts quickly added that sightings are not things of the past. They continue to occur and are reported to the authors by phone, through mail and e-mail correspondence and in person.

Jim related the story of a woman who approached the two men in the late 1990s at the New Jersey Folk Festival. She swore that she had seen a creature that was "hopping like a kangaroo." Recalling the conversation, Jim said, "I remember she told me, 'Put me in the book, 'cause I saw it!'"

The joy of the project, the authors agreed, is not only in writing the books.

"What I like," Jim said, "is to keep collecting stories and meeting the people, and visiting the Pine Barrens in New Jersey."

"This is interesting," Ray added, "because it is both a research project and a phenomenon. You can see how something supernatural or unexplained has become associated with popular culture, much like the story of the Loch Ness monster."

They also are pleased with the feedback they have received. Ray mentioned that the books are used in schools and libraries across the state to teach history and folklore. Also, he said it's been satisfying that both general interest readers and members of the academic community have accepted the work.

Awareness of the Jersey Devil certainly has increased following the popularity of the two books on the topic. However, conversations about the supernatural creature can develop rather unexpectedly.

While the authors were traveling in New Jersey, Ray said his car broke down and a state trooper arrived to render assistance. During their conversation, Ray and Jim mentioned their work on the state creature and the trooper gave the authors several new leads— one of the South Jersey Chicken Man plus information on other paranormal incidents in the region.

The biggest recent surge of publicity was associated with the release of the movie *13th Child: The Legend of the Jersey Devil*. The low-budget flick was released in October 2002 and starred Cliff Robertson.

When the well-known actor visited Philadelphia to promote the film's release, Ray attended a publici-

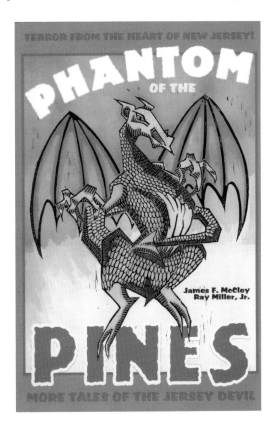

ty event and got to talk with the Hollywood star and the screenplay writer Mike Maryk.

"Our book inspired the movie," Jim said. "As a result, our publisher put out a new cover that reflects the connection. That had a direct effect on sales during the last quarter of the year."

Of course, dealing in such an unusual area of research and writing has caused a fair share of unusual experiences.

Their immediate reactions indicated that both men had stories to share.

For Jim the best tale occurred when his cousin, a missionary, was working in Africa. While in a remote valley in the bush country of Zimbabwe, Jim said, his relative ran into a fellow with a British accent. As soon as the Brit heard that the missionary's last name was McCloy, he asked, "Are you related to that guy who wrote *The Jersey Devil?*"

Ray said he heard from a fellow on the other end of the Earth, in Hawaii, who suggested that the Devil's story might fit in well with Polynesian legends and beliefs.

"Then there was the time we got reviewed in a British journal," Jim said, smiling. "They said we were out, literally with nets, trying to physically capture it."

Of course, one has to drop the big question: Do Jim and Ray believe in the Jersey Devil?

> '*It's more fun if you don't find it. That's what keeps it going. If they said they found that the Loch Ness monster was really a log, that would kill all the mystique. The search is more fun than finding the answer.*'
>
> —*Jim McCloy*

After the two authors traded hesitant glances across the table, Jim answered first. "There's certainly something out there that has kept the story going."

Smiling before he answered, Ray replied, "I used to say, 'If you ask me on Monday, Wednesday and Friday, the answer is no. But on Tuesday, Thursday, Saturday and Sunday, the answer is yes.' But that used to get me into trouble."

Shifting into a more serious tone, Ray added, "Some people say it's mass hysteria, and a percentage say there is something unexplained out there. The stories drive the imagination and the legend. But there's something out there in the Pine Barrens. We've seen the footprints and heard the reports that just can't be explained."

"But," Jim stressed, "it's more fun if you don't find it. That's what keeps it going. If they said they found that the Loch Ness monster was really a log, that would kill all the mystique. The search is more fun than finding the answer."

Author's note: To contact the authors, send an e-mail message to Jim McCloy at [gingergmm@aol.com] or to Ray Miller at [rmiller@udel.edu]. For information on their books, contact Middle Atlantic Press at 800 257-8481.

More than Kielbasa

Some of the best things in life are hidden away, off the beaten path, known only to those who take the time to search them out or who are "in the know." Along a narrow side street in the heart of Wilmington's Browntown section, an old building that used to be the home of West End Dairy sells the best Polish kielbasa between Warsaw and Chicago.

That's what the regular customers of Delaware Provision Company will tell you, and who's to say they're wrong?

Owner Sam "Scotty" Lavery is a butcher. Like the baker and candlestick maker, his occupation is something that today you only read about in fairy tales. Not many people in the 21st-century job market are scanning the want ads hoping to land any of those three occupations.

But up until the mid 1960s, neighborhood grocery stores were located on almost every city block. And the owners would prepare, cut and spice their own meats, selling the finished product to regular customers who would patronize their shops, often only buying enough food for a day or two. Then they would return to their favorite corner store a few days later.

How a Scotsman ended up being the last butcher in Delaware to make Polish meat products is the story of an enterprising immigrant chasing the American Dream and being in the right place at the right time.

In 1964, when he was 20 years old, Scotty came to America to live with his sister, who had previously arrived in Delaware. He said he came to pursue better opportunities. Within a year-and-a half he was drafted and serving a year in Vietnam.

After returning home in 1967, he worked at General Motors and then opened a food distribution company, selling products to small grocery stores. In the 1970s, he learned that Herman Barczewski, a well-known local grocer and butcher, was interested in selling his business and, more importantly, his Polish meat products recipes.

"I knew nothing about the business," Scotty said, recalling the days in 1980 when he and his wife, Kathy, considered getting into the meat business. But, with Herman agreeing to share his knowledge and teach the basics, Scotty bought the Barczewski meat business, special recipes and all. That was more than 20 years ago, and the times have changed dramatically since then.

Scotty said Herman could see how the corner grocery stores were dying out, and when they died out, so would the outlets for his meat products. But, what actually occurred is rather interesting.

Today, rather than having the customers go to the small stores to get their holiday and special meat products; they come directly to the factory—Scotty's business at 318 8th Avenue.

Sam 'Scotty' Lavery

Wilmington, Delaware

A flier lists a complete menu, offering kielbasa (smoked and fresh), kiszka, breakfast sausage, hamburgers, Italian sausage, sandwich steak, sauerkraut, meatballs, the list goes on and on.

"Christmas and Easter are our busiest times of year," Scotty said. "At Christmas, people are six deep all the way out to the gate. They wait for two-and-a-half hours for the products, and they see their friends in line and they don't seem to mind. It's like a reunion. People look forward to it. The waiting in line is part of the tradition."

One of the things that Scotty added to the business is catering. His wife, Kathy, takes care of all the scheduling, but people now order prepared meals for family events, including christenings, graduations, weddings, anniversaries, birthdays and funerals—as well as Super Bowl parties and reunions.

Scotty and Billy Hayes Jr.

Delaware Provision's catering business has taken off and is busy throughout the year because people are too busy to prepare food for large gatherings. With two parents working and fewer families continuing the tradition of contributing shared dishes to family events, they order from Scotty's 18-item menu, with such selections as pasta salad and cole slaw, baked ziti, pepper steak, spezzato and kielbasa and kraut.

"All of our business is from word of mouth," Scotty said, "satisfied customers. We do everything from christenings to funerals, from the cradle to the grave."

But as the years pass it's natural to assume that many of his regular customers are dying off.

True, Scotty agreed, but there's a strong representation from the younger generations.

"The younger people remember, and they like, their Christmas traditions," Scotty said. "They like the holidays being back like they were. They want

their butter lambs and they want the food that they had when they were young. It reminds them of their parents and grandparents. It's part of the nostalgia."

After 23 years, Scotty is looking toward the future, and a member of the next generation has been learning the meat business for the last four years. Scotty's nephew, 20-year-old Billy Hayes Jr., will take over when Scotty is ready to hang up his apron.

"I love this business," Scotty said, surveying his shop. "I love interacting with the people."

Suddenly, a grin spread across his face. It was obvious that he wanted to share another thought or two.

"People wonder why a Scotsman had become the last of the kielbasa makers in the area," Scotty said, his subtle Old World accent becoming a bit more pronounced. "But no one else is doing it. You have to go to Philadelphia or Baltimore to get the real Polish sausage and meats now.

"We get people who come back here to the area from California, expatriates, and a lot from Florida. They make us a regular stop and load up on kielbasa and take it wherever they're going. That happens often.

"But the days of the old neighborhood stores are gone. Even in Philadelphia there are only a handful. It's not just here. It's all over the country. There was a time when every corner had a store and everyone cut meat. Now, we're the last of our kind. You can count on your hand the number of butchers around, so you can't pick and choose any longer. It's amazing how lifestyles have changed in the last 20 years."

Author's note: To contact Delaware Provision Company, call (302) 429-0220 or (302) 658-6037.

Photograph by Jack Buxbaum, University of Delaware

Ron Whittington

Wilmington, Delaware

Making Baseball History

When a friend of Ron Whittington asked him to don a Civil War uniform, he had no idea where the experience would lead him. Initially, the idea was to try out for an extra in the movie *Glory*. Ron—who works at the University of Delaware as special assistant to the dean of the College of Human Resources, Education and Public Policy—didn' t get the part, but the experience deepened his interest in the contributions of black soldiers to the Union cause.

Eventually, Ron would become a performer on the National Chautauqua Tour, an organization that offers presentations about local and national historic figures across the United States. This interest in history also has gotten Ron an invitation to make a presentation at the Baseball Hall of Fame and Museum in Cooperstown, New York.

Ron' s first experience as an historical performer began a few years back, while visiting an exhibit about Delaware during the Civil War that was being presented by the Historical Society of Delaware.

"I was looking at the list of black men from Delaware who had fought in the war, and I came across the name of William Owen, a freed black man from Milford, " Ron said. "He was 36 years old at the time, and he was in Wilmington to hear Frederick Douglass speak at the house of Thomas Garrett. "

Garrett was a Wilmington abolitionist who helped

> *'I also try to tell them that these guys were real-life heroes—people who played for the love of the game—not just for the money.'*
>
> —Ron Whittington

many blacks gain their freedom. Among them was Douglass, who Garrett had spirited up the Delaware River to Philadelphia.

Owen eventually enlisted with the Union Army as part of the 54th Massachusetts Regiment, one of the many black regiments that saw action during the war.

Ron developed a program portraying Owens in a presentation of *A House Divided*, written by Tom Reed, of New Castle. The play, which explored the conflicting loyalties of Delawareans during the Civil War, featured a roundtable discussion of four historical figures.

In addition to Owen, the discussion included Union Capt. Rickets, who returned to Delaware after being wounded at Fredericksburg; a Confederate soldier and member of Mosby' s Rangers, named John Dunning; and Rev. Isaac Handy, a retired minister from Port Penn, Delaware, who was a prisoner at Fort Delaware.

"The play showed the many conflicts that existed in the country, " Ron said. "It also is a reminder of the significant role Delaware played in the conflict, including the use of Wilmington as a major Union port and the functioning of Fort Delaware as a Union prison. "

As Ron, a high school and college athlete, became comfortable in his new performing role, another opportunity surfaced—and the source of the inspiration was much closer to home.

One of the top players in the old Negro League was the late Judy Johnson, Delaware's only member of the Baseball Hall of Fame inducted as a player.

When Ron's friends heard he was looking for a character to portray on the National Chautauqua Tour, they told him stories about Judy Johnson. In the days just after the World War I, the black athlete played ball in the neighborhood around Lancaster Avenue, near DuPont and Clayton streets. When Ron was playing baseball, he met Judy when the retired Hall of Famer was scouting for the Philadelphia Phillies.

"After I had just hit a long home run to right center, Judy came up and congratulated me," Ron recalled. "Then, he asked me why I didn't pull the ball."

Judy, Ron explained, was trying to explain that

Ron in his role as a Civil War soldier

to move up a notch or two, the young athlete would have to learn how to swing with his hips. It turned out Judy was right, for while Ron did go on to play semipro baseball, he said he never progressed to the next level.

When Ron decided to portray the local baseball legend, he said he was determined to get things right historically. Ron got theatrical help from Sandy Robbins, Barbara Lampros-Hughes and Joan Nardo of the University of Delaware's Professional Theatre Training Program, and he received other contributions from Wilmington Blue Rocks owner Matt Minker and UD professor of English and baseball book author Kevin Kerrane. By the summer of 2000, with all his props in place, he began offering presentations locally and across the country, in such diverse locales as Oklahoma City, Philadelphia and the Negro League Museum in Kansas City.

Ron also shares with youngsters the history and heritage of other Negro League stars, like Josh Gibson and Leroy "Satchel" Paige.

"When I talk to the young people, I try to answer their questions in the manner in which Judy Johnson would talk to them today," Ron said. "I also try to tell them that these guys were real-life heroes— people who played for the love of the game—not just for the money."

Although Judy Johnson, who was born in Snow Hill, Maryland, is the only First State player to gain official entry to the Baseball Hall of Fame in Cooperstown, that shrine of baseball glory has opened its door to Ron on several occasions.

In the summer of 2002, Ron and friend Chuck Chalberg teamed up to do a presentation about Branch Rickey and Jackie Robinson. Once again a debate served as the forum as Ron and Chuck, in character as Robinson and Rickey, debated the issue of why Rickey picked Robinson over Monte Irvin to break baseball's color barrier in 1947.

Ron's slide show about baseball and Judy Johnson has been accepted by Cooperstown and works well, he said, in the museum's sandlot story forum.

Photograph by Kathy F. Atkinson, University of Delaware

One of the neat things about getting invited to Cooperstown, Ron said, is that once your presentation if finished, you can come back and tour the museum after it has closed to the general public. "We went back three nights in a row," Ron remembered. He also enjoyed watching the many baseball tournaments that seem to be going on all summer around the grounds at Cooperstown.

"I saw a 78-year old guy steal a base during one of the games," Ron said, smiling. "How often do you see that?"

Ron said his main concern is connecting to his audience wherever he happens to be performing.

"The audience at Cooperstown was amazing," Ron said. "They ranged from kids in strollers to grandparents with their canes."

Whether it is the presentation of new characters, such as Marcus Garvey, the Jamaican-born charismatic black leader who organized America's first black nationalistic movement in Harlem during the 1920s, or Civil War solder William Owen, Ron said he enjoys having people come up to him after a performance to share stories of their own.

"At first, before you take the stage, you have a little nervousness, but once you get past that point, you start to connect with the crowd," Ron said. "I enjoy the reaction of the people, especially the kids."

One thing Ron likes to share is a quote from Judy Johnson. Before the end of each of his programs Ron, as Judy, tells his audience, "Somewhere the sun is shinning—and they are playing a ball game."

—*Jerry Rhodes*

Author's note: To contact Ron Whittington, call him at (302) 658-5993 or send him an e-mail message at [rwhitt@udel.edu].

Another version of this story appeared in *UpDate*, the University of Delaware's faculty and staff newspaper.

Chuck Wehrle

Elkton, Maryland

Photographing D-Day

It's an ordinary house, not very different from hundreds of others along tree-lined streets near Old Field Point Road, just east of Elkton, Maryland. Well-kept driveways are accented with a scattering of American flags. Kids arriving home from school carry bookbags and basketballs tucked under their arms.

A green Ford Taurus sits in the driveway of the home of Chuck and Catherine Wehrle. On the rear bumper, a very small blue rectangular sticker with white lettering states: "I Did 'D' Day, 6th June '44."

Other than that, there's no clue that 59 years ago, the tall, 78-year-old retiree—just your average man next door—played a role in recording one of history's greatest wartime events on the beaches of Normandy. And, a year later, he photographed the ending days of the war in the jungles of the South Pacific and the atomic devastation in Nagasaki.

Chuck Wehrle, in August 1944, after returning from duty in Europe

Photograph provided by Chuck Wehrle, from his private collection

"I was only 19 years old when I made D-Day," Chuck said, seated on a couch in what he said his children call the "War Room." Photographs of a much younger man in a U.S. Coast Guard uniform look down from the walls. In a few photos he is alone, in others he is smiling beside a few close wartime buddies. Another frame holds his medals, including a Purple Heart.

Rising from his seat, the veteran gets up to point to a group of seven young men, most of them passed away—all U.S. Coast Guard photographers. All were there with cameras in hand on D-Day.

As he returns to his seat to share his memories, you get a sense that Chuck can see it all again, the frantic mission preparations, the chaotic landing, the horrifying aftermath on the beaches and bluffs. His training and skills as a photographers mate allow him to visualize the events that he saw through his lens, the history that he captured on film nearly six decades ago.

It doesn't seem that long," Chuck said. "The first 50 years, they went by very quickly. I never talked about the war. I don't know why. You were young and crazy and took some chances back then. I never thought something would happen to me. I always thought I would come home. But I wanted to come home to the life I had, hanging out with my friends, singing, playing cards, going to the clubs. But when I came back, it wasn't the same place. Things had changed."

A major adjustment, Chuck said, was attending weddings nearly every weekend of war pals and neighborhood friends. At one of these nuptials, Chuck said

he met Catherine, who was there as a bridesmaid. They were married in 1947, and they have five children, Chuck Jr., David, Mark, Christine and Janis. Originally from Philadelphia, Chuck and Catherine raised their children in New Jersey. In the 1980s, they often drove to Cecil County of to see one of their children who had moved into the area.

While visiting they saw a house for sale, and on Flag Day, June 14, 1990, the Wehrles moved into Arundel and became county residents.

In 1994, D-Day veteran Donnie Preston of North East invited Chuck to a special ceremony planned to recognize Cecil County veterans who had been involved in the Normandy landings.

"On the way to the car," Chuck recalled, "my oldest son, Chuck Jr., said, 'Dad. You never talked about the war. You didn't even tell us which beach you were on.' "

That ceremony and the friendships that have developed with area veterans of the 29th Infantry Division have changed Chuck's life.

For the last several years, the war photographer has been a regular attendee of the bi-weekly meetings of the 29th Infantry Division in the Veterans of Foreign Wars Post in North East, Maryland. He's also been active with 101st Airborne veterans Joe Lofthouse of Elkton and Ralph Kelly of Aberdeen, delivering the message and experiences of D-Day to schools in Maryland and surrounding states.

Chuck said being invited to be a guest speaker at the Eisenhower National Historic Site in Gettysburg, Pennsylvania, two years in a row during the area's World War II Weekend was "an honor and a privilege I'll never forget."

Opening a copy of *World War II: A Photographic History*, a large, hardbound book by David Boyle, Chuck turned to page 219.

"That's my picture," he said, pointing to the photograph of supplies being delivered to Omaha Beach. Chuck said the picture is a very popular image and it has been featured in other books and periodicals.

Another of his pictures, taken on the beach a few days after the landing, is included on the top of page 220.

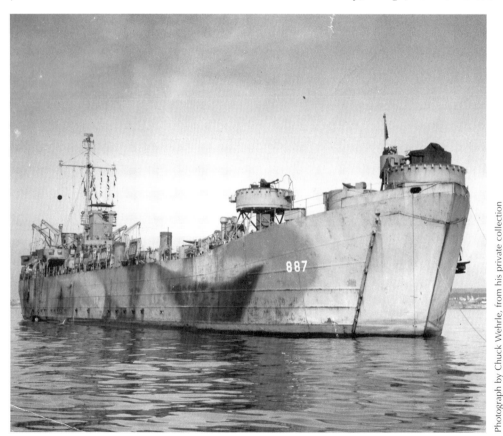

Photograph by Chuck Wehrle, from his private collection

LST 887, which Chuck referred to as "My Ship," was involved in the Okinawa Invasion and visit to Nagasaki, Japan, soon after the atomic blast.

As he flipped through the pages of another book, *American at D-Day*, by Richard Goldstein, Chuck described it was one of the best books he's ever found about the invasion. He also pointed out a famous image of troops exiting a landing craft taken by a fellow Coast Guard photographer.

"I feel pretty good," Chuck said, "that three or four of the best ones taken at D-Day were taken by U. S. Coast Guard photographers."

"I carried five cameras with me," Chuck said. "We'd take them [shot film] and go to the radio room on the ship, where it would be radioed in for pick up. I never saw it after I sent it in."

Chuck said the photographers in the field never did any processing. That was done in laboratories, where staff would develop the film, make prints and select the pictures that would be sent to newspapers and magazines around the world. There would be 150 copies of each of the best pictures distributed for release. However, although no name credit was given to individual photographers, Chuck said he and his fellow photographers mates knew which pictures were theirs.

Chuck recalled that the trip across the English Channel was about 100 miles to The Far Shore. "That's what we used to call France when we spoke of it, The Far Shore."

He said the convoy of Navy ships, troop transports and amphibious ships numbered in the thousands. "Later in the morning," Chuck said, "when the airmen flew over, they said it looked like you could step from ship to ship. The overall operation had the code name Overlord. The naval portion, with all of our ships, was called Operation Neptune."

Chuck said he landed on Omaha and shot roll after roll of film.

"Some people asked me how many pictures I took that day," he said. "I cannot remember how many pictures I shot that day. All I can say is that no matter what direction you pointed your camera, you took a picture of history being made around you. I was very proud of us seven [U. S. Coast Guard] photographers in this flotilla."

Chuck said one of the pictures taken by a member of his group—S. Scott Wigle, former Detroit journalist—was the first D-Day photo transmitted by military authorities to newspapers in the United States.

"It showed the LCI's [Landing Craft Infantry] crossing the English Channel with the barrage balloons above them. The camera was later sold for $8-1/2 million in war bond purchases during the national broadcast Victory Bond Auction. Many of

Damage from a suicide plane on a Sunday morning in Okinawa

Photograph by Chuck Wehrle, from his private collection

the photos that the rest of us took are in the National Archives today, and we are all very proud of them."

Chuck's experiences during the war could fill volumes. He described the pictures he took: Allied soldiers, German prisoners, mine holes in destroyed landing craft (that he described as "burnt out coffins"), dead bodies that littered the beach, heavy equipment arriving to build port facilities that would accept the stream of more men and equipment needed for the Allied march to Berlin. All the action was caught on film and all the memories are imprinted in his mind.

While acknowledging the bravery during the invasions in North Africa, Sicily and Italy, Chuck explained why he still believes the Normandy landing was so important and receives so much attention.

"D-Day is one of the biggest invasions," he said. "The war had been going on for quite a few years.

> *'I cannot remember how many pictures I shot that day. All I can say is that no matter what direction you pointed your camera, you took a picture of history being made around you.'*
> —*Chuck Wehrle*

But it was only 11 months after D-Day that the Axis was done. From June 6 to May 8. The Russians wanted a second front and that was it. It was the beginning of the end of the war. Rommel said, 'If we can't stop them at the beach, we're going to lose the war.' I often wonder what would have happened if we didn't move off that beach and advance forward."

Like many Americans, Chuck saw the movie *Saving Private Ryan.*

"I thought it was very impressive," the veteran said. "When it started, I got tears in my eyes and walked to the back of the theater. It was very impressive. But, if they actually showed what really happened, some of the photographs, you wouldn't believe it."

Although he said the beginning of the movie was quite realistic, he said some of the heroics and daredevil scenes at the end were "unrealistic" and "pure Hollywood."

In July 1944, Chuck was ordered back to Washington, D.C., to supervise a photographic laboratory, but he soon applied for transfer to the front. By September, and with a promotion to photographers mate second class, he was heading to the South Pacific. "I was on my way again," Chuck said, smiling.

In April 1945, Chuck took part in the invasion of Okinawa. Later that year, after the peace terms were signed on the battleship USS *Missouri*, he

Photograph provied by Chuck Wehrle, from his private collection

U.S. Coast Guard photographers sent to cover the Okinawa Invasion. Not one had reached the age of 21. Chuck Wehrle is second from right, and his friend and fellow D-Day photographer Harold Barclay, is second from left.

was among the first American servicemen to walk the streets of Nagasaki, target of the second atomic bomb.

"Looking around," Chuck said, "it's a sight that I will never forget for as long as I live. Everything that used to be green—the trees, the bushes, everything—was a golden brown.

"Being a photographer, I went ashore. I went down to the shipyard where they made the one-man and two-man subs. The steel girders that contained the cranes that would transport these little subs after they were made were melted and twisted into such shapes that you would never believe. And, this was miles from the blast."

Occasionally, Chuck said, when he is wearing a World War II baseball cap or VFW attire, passers-by will thank him for his service to the country.

"I've had people eating in McDonald's come up and say, 'I just want to thank you for what you have done for us.' That doesn't happen too often," Chuck said, "but when it does, it makes you feel good."

His fellow WW II Coast Guard photographer Harold Barclay contacted Chuck to tell him that they each have a photograph displayed at the National D-Day Museum in New Orleans. Chuck smiled at the thought, then added that he didn't know if he would ever travel that far south to see his photograph on exhibit.

Chuck left the service at the rank of photographers mate first class. In his War Room are boxes of photographs and newspaper clippings waiting to be organized and placed in keepsake albums. But after listening to the D-Day veteran, it's doubtful he needs to rely on such mementoes to spark memories that seem so vivid and clear, even after nearly 60 years.

"My kids ask me if I ever shot anybody during the war," Chuck said. "I tell them, 'Yeah! I shot thousands of them—with my camera.'"

Author's note: A similar version of this story first appeared in *The Cecil Whig.*

Vicki, Nancy and Les Pearson

Stanton, Delaware

Specializing in Red, White & Blue

What do a loaf of bread, a key cutting machine and thousands of flags have in common? For nearly six decades, all these items have been sold across the counter of a small family business, located in a one-story building in Stanton, Delaware.

Les, 76, and Nancy Pearson, 71, and their daughter, Vicki, 41, operate Pearson's Suburban Flag Headquarters, which is one of the best-known and most active flag selling shops in the mid-Atlantic region.

Their success story began years ago, in 1948, when Nancy's parents, James and Alice Maclary, opened a grocery store named Maclary's Market at the site. In 1956, Les and Nancy took over half the building to operate a small hardware store. Two years later, the young couple was using the entire building and put up a sign proclaiming Pearson Hardware.

That was in 1958. Now, 45 years later, on a winter afternoon in the 21st century, the three members of the staff gathered in the front of the shop to talk about old times. Nancy paused and smiled at Les, who was seated at his usual spot behind the front counter.

It was obvious that Nancy enjoyed sharing the legend about how a grocery/hardware store was transformed into a major flag/souvenir outlet.

"Les had a blue Delaware hat, with the motto 'Small Wonder,' which he hung over a rack near the cash register," Nancy recalled. "Customers would say, 'I'll take two of those hats.' I told Les that he would either have to take the hat down or we'd have to start selling them."

Today, the aisles of the former grocery/hardware are filled with stacks of goods and merchandise. But the bins that held nuts and bolts and the shelves that contained bread and cereal now offer Delaware memorabilia and flags of every imaginable type and size.

First-time visitors scanning the interior of this unique family enterprise have trouble focusing their attention. On the right side of the shop are aisles displaying flags—military service types, U. S., Civil War, foreign countries. They sit beside Delaware books, clothing, lighters, key chains, baseball caps, plates, calendars, decorative license plates . . . and much much more. You get the idea.

On the other end of the building are more and more flags, and the back wall presents a rainbow-colored display of banners—featuring different pets, various holidays, all the seasons of the year, plus sailboats and lighthouses and flowers, and more.

Then there are the floor mats and windsocks. Oh, and in the side room are the sports flags, banners and items, each bearing the emblem of a customer's favorite team, whether it's the Eagles, Redskins, Flyers, Phillies, or a team located thousands of miles across the country. You name it, they've got it.

But don't forget the college team merchandise and all-important flagpoles—in-ground, porch-type and automobile style—to display the banners.

When asked how many items are in the shop, Nancy turned to Les, who shrugged his shoulders and replied, "Lots!" When pressed, she and her husband and Vicki agreed that there were many thousands of flags and many hundreds of Delaware souvenirs.

The flags alone range from tiny, hand-held and desktop models measured in inches, to giant, full-size, 20-feet by 30-feet versions of Old Glory that fly high above car dealerships and at military sites.

The big push to offer more flags occurred in the early 1990s, during Operation Desert Storm, Nancy and Les said. People were standing up and down the aisles, grabbing whatever they could that was red, white and blue.

In the fall of 1999, flooding from Hurricane Floyd filled the shop with several feet of water. After that, whatever remained of the hardware in the Pearson store was not replaced, and flags and souvenirs took over the entire building.

Within hours after the 9/11 tragedies occurred, the Pearson's shop was the site of a mad rush by persons interested in buying patriotic symbols. Outside the store traffic jammed the street and inside a mob of customers filled the building.

"It was unbelievable," Nancy said. "You couldn't look up to wait on the people."

"You couldn't park anywhere," Les said, shaking his head at the memory. "You would try to close and people were banging on the door."

Vicki said it was so crowded that the line at the cash register extended through the store. "I was walking up and down the aisles, taking cash and rounding off what they owed in my head. One woman gave me her money and then asked, 'Now, you really do work here don't you?' "

"It was like that for three or four days," Les said. "We were mobbed. They were grabbing anything that looked like an American flag. Russian flags. Historical flags. Libya. Liberia. Anything with red, white and blue. The shelves were empty."

One of the funniest incidents occurred a few days after September 11, when a woman walked into Pearsons to return an American flag that she announced was the wrong size.

"A whole line of people started bidding on her flag," Nancy said. "We had hardly nothing left and they were glad to take it off her hands. It cost $24.95. I think it got up to $50 for it. She sold it to someone in line. She never returned it to us."

From his seat behind the front counter where he works seven days a week, Les said, "We were exhausted. We were here all day long and we never had time to look up or talk to the people. It was like we were on an assembly line. The charge machine never got a chance to rest. We never had a chance to restock, eventually there was nothing left to put on the shelves."

With the phone constantly ringing, Nancy said all she could do was pick up the receiver, and say, "We don't have any flags!"

Rolling her eyes, she added, "I didn't even say, 'Pearsons.' "

And while it's expected that wars and national tragedies will cause lines to form at the flag store,

Maclary's Market and Pearson's Hardware Store in the 1950s

Photograph provided by Les and Nancy Pearson, from their collection

the Pearsons said their business is steady and strong throughout the entire year.

When he was young, Les said, people used to fly the flag on Memorial Day and on July Fourth, and those flags lasted for years. Today, many people raise their flags every day, and eventually the material fades and the flag wears out. As a result, one-time buyers become regular customers.

Vicki, who came to work in the family business a few years ago, said some of the best stories are related to the Delaware souvenir side of the family business.

She mentioned the tale of a woman who bought a Delaware "Small Wonder" baseball cap before she left to attend the Olympics in Australia. While Down Under in Sydney, the woman was walking down the street and saw a man coming toward her—and he was wearing the exact same style Delaware cap.

"When they met," Vicki said, "they started talking and found out that they lived within a few miles of each other and they both had bought their caps right here, in our store. And they met each other in Australia!"

Only those who have been involved in a family business can truly understand the special relationship among the owners, and the sense of pride they share in maintaining their independence. It's hard work, but very satisfying.

"I like the interaction with the customers," Vicki said. "And I've always been close with my mom, but now, working five days a week in the store, I've gotten closer with my dad. That's a nice benefit of working here."

When asked what she likes about the business, Nancy had a reply ready. "I like it because of the people I meet," she said.

"Everybody who comes in is happy. When they're picking out flags and banners, they are doing

something to beautify their home. When we were in the hardware business, everybody who came in had problems. They were grouchy because they had to fix something, or the men were mad because the wife wanted them to paint a room, or they had to do yard work."

But then there's the story of the bread, and the keys.

"Ten years after the grocery had been closed and we were into the hardware business, people came in and wanted to know where the bread was," Nancy said. "But even today, with the hardware gone since 1999, people will come in and ask to have their keys cut. And we tell them we took the key machine out years ago. But they say, 'I get my keys cut here all the time.'"

Author's note: For information on all types of flags and Delaware souvenirs, clothing and books, call Les, Nancy or Vicki at (302) 994-4281 or send an e-mail note to [flags2125@aol.com].

Les Pearson near some of the flags in his store

Photograph by Christopher Cook

John Russell

Wilmington, Delaware

Taking Care of Typewriters

When John Russell went to work for Hilyard's Inc. a business machine company, after graduating from Salesanium High School in 1959, typewriters ruled the roost.

Computers were something from science fiction movies—they took a lot of space and sat behind locked doors in university labs and secret government buildings. They ate cards filled with square holes and were attended by serious minded academic types who wore long white coats and carried around something called a slide rule.

Russell, who retired from full time duties after 43 years of service with the networking solutions and document imaging firm located near Prices Corner, remembered what it was like when he started there as an apprentice.

"Charles Hilyard had just started the business. They had one service tech and two salesmen, and were looking for an apprentice," John said. "We were so small that we used to work on anything from cash registers to mimeograph machines."

And typewriters.

When John started at Hilyard's, the firm was located on West Eight Street, not far from the old *News Journal* newspaper building, between Shipley and Orange. In those days, Hilyard's was a distributor for Olympia typewriters.

After learning as much as he could from the service manager, John spent a year at the Olympia training school in New York City.

In those early years after finishing his technical training in the Big Apple, John said he worked mainly on manual typewriters, which were still pretty popular. It was not unusual, John said, for Hilyard's to sell up to 200 typewriters during the Christmas holidays.

In the 1960s, John recalled, he worked on typewriters that were made in the early 1900s. Today, it's rare to come across anything that old, but he still gets requests to repair and service manual models made in the 1940s.

As a service technician, John said he received just one complaint from a customer during all his years with the firm. However, he does recall some very interesting on-site calls that he made as someone fairly new in the trade.

"I was sent to Padua Academy, and was working on a typewriter in the typing classroom, when a nun came in and said, 'What are you doing in here young man?'" Russell recalled. "I guess she didn't like the idea of a young guy like me, just out of high school, being around all those girls."

While the good sister proved quite amenable when she learned the official nature of John's visit, other customers were not quite so understanding.

"I remember going on my first service call, and I wanted to make a really good impression," John said.

> 'People are shocked when they find out what I do. They are very surprised that there are still typewriters out there. Some people say, "Thank God there's someone like you who can repair them." '
>
> —John Russell

"I knocked on the door, and a woman opened it. I told her I was here to fix Mr. Smith's typewriter. 'He's dead!' the woman said. I guess I didn't hear her, because I told her one more time that I was there to fix Mr. Smith's typewriter.

"The woman gave me a hard look, and said, 'You don't understand—he's dead.' I said, 'Do you still want your typewriter fixed?' Then, she slammed the door in my face."

While John was learning the ins-and-outs of customer service, the manual typewriter was about to be replaced during the mid-1960s with something call the IBM Selectric. It was this machine, John said, that "revolutionized the typewriter industry."

During the late 1970s, Olympia improved its product, and the electronic typewriter boom of the 1980s, led by IBM, was underway. It seemed like every office had one of these machines, and John remembered that Hilyard's had four service technicians who worked almost exclusively on what was considered the cutting-edge office machine of the time.

"The electronics were completely different from the older machines, in that they required very little cleaning and very little lubricating," John said. "They also were very complicated, but once you got to know how the machines worked, they were easier to work on than the older typewriters."

Although the electronic typewriters were enjoying a long golden summer before the arrival of the personal computer in the early 1990s, there were many new products appearing on the market that required occasional servicing.

Among these products were hand-held calculators that came out in the early 1970s. They cost about $250 and could add, subtract, multiply and divide, but not much more, Russell recalled. They were, however, extremely popular.

"There were a lot of mechanical parts on the early ones, and we had one man in the early 1970s who did nothing but work on calculators," John said. "He did this for about 15 years."

While 80 percent of his time was spent working on typewriters, John said he also learned the ins and outs of dictating and folding machines, shredders, binders, cutters and duplicating machines. He also attended schools for each piece of equipment he would have to fix. He studied cash registers in Detroit, typewriters in New York City, Baltimore, Lancaster, Kansas City and Philadelphia, mimeograph machines in Atlanta, copiers on Long Island and calculators in Washington.

The toughest job, John recalls, was working on the massive copiers used by large corporations, because they were very complicated, and office managers were under a great deal of pressure to keep their copiers running.

Although the technological revolution would soon be marketing a product that would dethrone the venerable typewriter, John

John Russell at work on an old typewriter

said the staff found many of the new products interesting and enjoyed working on them.

"We thought that all that new stuff, like the fax machines that came out in the mid-1980s, were really something," John said. "They were big and expensive, and used thermal paper. Just the concept that you could fax things over a phone line was very interesting to us."

With the arrival of the personal computer in the early 1990s, typewriter sales started a long, steady decline, and with it went a corresponding loss in the number of calls to service the machines.

"By 1998, I was the only person working on them. Now, I get about five service calls a week," said John, who added that people are amazed when they find out that in this modern, high tech age, he still gets calls to repair typewriters.

"People are shocked when they find out what I do," John admitted. "They are very surprised that there are still typewriters out there. I tell them there are thousands of them out there. Some people say, 'Thank God there's someone like you who can repair them.' "

Although he recently retired from full-time duties at Hilyard's, John said there's still enough business to keep him busy 10 to 12 hours a week—the rest of the time he tries to get in some bass fishing in the Chesapeake Bay or on one of it tributaries.

John said people don't realize the number of typewriters still being used in places like school districts, law offices and banks. Many places use the machines to fill in forms that are just too time consuming to perform on a personal computer.

And there are those loyal aficionados who cling passionately to their favorite Olympia, Remington or Selectric and refuse to give them up.

"They have sentimental value to a lot of people. Some used them at work and others received them as gifts," John said. "A lot of people love their old typewriters. It's just something they grew up with."

—*Jerry Rhodes*

Author's note: To contact John, call Hilyard's Inc. at (302) 995-2201.

Photograph by Larry Foster

'Chubby' Imburgia
Claymont, Delaware

Working on the Chain Gang

It took Joseph "Chubby" Imburgia almost 61 years to make it to the National Football League—but he's enjoyed every minute of it since then.

The Marcus Hook, Pennsylvania, native, and longtime resident of Claymont, in northern Delaware, doesn't pass, run, tackle or coach. But his work on the sidelines is just as important in the eyes of the officials, whose job is to see that some of the toughest guys in shoulder pads play by the rules during Philadelphia Eagles home games.

Chubby talks about his part-time job with all the enthusiasm of a kid suiting up for his first high school football game. As the "drive pole guy" his job is to mark the beginning spot of each team's possession with the football. No matter how far down the field the team advances through each series of first downs, Chubby remains at the spot where the series began.

"One time a punter came over to me," Chubby recalled, "and he told me, 'The two loneliest men in the NFL are the team punter and guy who holds the drive pole.'"

Chubby retired in 1989 after a 38-year career with Sun Oil Company in Marcus Hook (his dad worked there 52 years). He got the much-sought-after chain gang job through a meeting in 1992 with Harry Gamble, then general manager of the Eagles.

"I went to a Pennsylvania Sports Hall of Fame luncheon, where I met Harry Gamble," Chubby said. "I got a tip from one of my friends that Harry was going to be there."

What Chubby did was simply slip Harry a letter expressing his desire to become part of the crew that moves the chains during games at Veterans Stadium, the Eagles home field.

"In the letter, I told Harry that like Martin Luther King Jr., 'I had a dream.' My dream as a youngster was getting a football scholarship and playing in college and then making it to the pros," Chubby said. "I also told Harry that because of work and family obligations, plus a two-year hitch in the Army during the Korean War, I was not able to do that."

The next thing Chubby knew, he received a letter from the Eagles requesting a resume.

In his response, Chubby told about his work as a volunteer for the United Way and the MacDonald's Ladies Professional Golfing Association Championship, held each year at the DuPont Country Club. He also noted his 40 years of refereeing high school football games in Pennsylvania, Maryland and Delaware.

Perhaps the most important thing Chubby wrote was the fact that he didn't run very well.

"I got a call from Mimi Box, who was vice-president in charge of finance for the team," Chubby remembered. "She told me that she wanted to meet me so she could put a face with my application."

She also told Chubby that she was very impressed with his honesty, especially the part about his not being able to run as well as he would like. While Mimi was pondering whether to hire the retiree from Marcus Hook, Harry Gamble strolled into the room and put in a good word for the man he had met only recently.

"Harry told Mimi that he was just like me, as far as the running ability went," Chubby said. "He also said that the team could use a few more old-timers to make things run smoothly on the sidelines."

For Chubby, who knew he had landed the job when he received an invitation to come to the stadium for a training session, this was one of the greatest moments of his life. When he walked onto the field at the Vet, he said it seemed like a whole new world had just opened up before his eyes.

"I was like the character in the movie *Rudy*, who finally got the chance to play for Notre Dame after sitting on the bench for most of the season," Chubby said. "I had so much enthusiasm. I could have gone out on the field and played ball with the big guys."

At the time, Chubby had an extensive football background from decades of officiating and from playing guard for Eddystone High School. He also had enjoyed a 13-year semi-pro football career with the Marcus Hook Athletic Association. Still, he knew there was a lot he had to learn about this latest stage in his football odyssey.

Photograph by Larry Foster

Chubby, on the sideline during a cold day in Veterans' Stadium

"The first cold game I dressed like I do when I officiate high school games," Chubby said. "I soon learned that you had to dress like you were going hunting in winter time."

Chubby almost shivers when he recalls coldest game he ever worked at the Vet—the Jan. 12, 2003 playoff game between the Eagles and the Atlanta Falcons. "That was the coldest I've ever been," Chubby laughed. "I'm still cold from that game—and I've been down at the beach all summer.

"During another game in the cold," he said, smiling, "I moved too close to the big heaters they have on the sideline and my white pants caught on fire. I had so many layers of clothing on I didn't even notice it. A police officer came over and started beating on me, helping to put the fire out!"

What Chubby also learned, during his "rookie season of 1992," is that there is a certain routine to be followed—and there are no exceptions to the rules laid down by the team and the security personnel, who make sure only authorized folks gain access to the playing field.

Chubby said he arrives at the stadium about two hours before kickoff. Once allowed inside by security, he decides whether to head to the cafeteria in the stadium, where a nice buffet is spread out, or to stroll out on the field to see the local celebrities, who always seem to be on the field before each game.

Another must for chain crew members occurs an hour before the game when they attend a meeting presided over by the head linesman. He spells out the ground rules on how he wants the officiating and chain crew duties to be conducted.

Although Chubby described his place on the field as "one of the best spots in the stadium," he also said when the game is being played there is no time for daydreaming. "You have to be very careful and aware of everything that is going on out there," Chubby said.

"Once a defensive player came over and grabbed my pole," Chubby said. "He told me he wanted to see if I was awake. I told him, 'I'm more awake right here than you are out there on the field!'"

Chubby described his rule of thumb for getting out of the way when a gang of 250- pound- plus guys come running full speed toward the spot where he is standing.

"I tell the photographers, if you get in my way when I' m trying to get out of theirs, I' m going to run over you," Chubby said. "I've seen photographers get hit while trying to get that last shot. One time the guy carrying the pole got hit. It even bent the pole."

To keep things orderly on the sidelines, Chubby said, there is a person known as the "get- back coach." His job is to tell the players to literally *get back* from the area close to the sideline.

Sometimes, during a time out, Chubby said he might get a chance, however briefly, to talk to the players who happen to be in the area where he is standing. During a game against the Tampa Bay Buccaneers, Chubby asked one of the players where he went to high school.

"The guy told me he went to Christiana High School, in Delaware," Chubby said. "The guy was Jamie Duncan, and he told me to say hello to his friends down in the First State, including his high school coaches and *News Journal* sports reporter Matt Zabitka."

It is not unusual, Chubby noted, for friends to come down to the edge of the stands and call out to him before a game or during a break in the action. Another group of fans are not always happy that the guys working the chains are in the area.

"There is a section in the Vet where the seats are almost level with the field," Chubby said. "When we are standing in front of them, they yell for us to get out of the way so they can see the action. The things they yell are not very kind. But no matter what happens during the game, the players and management of the Eagles are always respectful of all of us on the chain gang."

When not working during Eagles' home games, Chubby keeps busy by officiating at high school football games. He is especially proud that he has been

working the annual Thanksgiving game between Sun Valley and Chichester high schools for 35 consecutive years.

"I have to give special credit to my wife, Norma, who has made allowances for me on weekends and holidays all these years," Chubby said. "I have had a lot of wonderful support from my family all these years."

Although he has been involved in football in some fashion since the 1940s, Chubby said each time he steps out onto the sidelines at the Vet he is just as thrilled as his he was during his first game in 1992 against the Chicago Bears.

Over the years, Chubby admitted, he's been asked hundreds of times—by everyone from high school coaches to strangers and friends—how he got the drive pole job.

"I think to myself, this is really something," Chubby said. "It's every kid's dream to be out there with the players and on the sidelines. I have made it all the way from Marcus Hook to the National Football League."

—*Jerry Rhodes*

Chubby, at a sports banquet with former Marcus Hook resident and pro football star Billy "White Shoes" Johnson

Folks
Down the Road

Photograph by Kathy F. Atkinson

Richard Humphreys

Kirkwood, Pennsylvania

Gnome Man's Land

Richard Humphreys isn't a gnome, he just dresses like one. The fact that he's a normal-sized adult is the hint that he's a gnome imposter. After all, everyone knows that genuine gnomes are little people—very, very little people.

Actually, Richard, 60, is the proprietor, guide, entertainer and teacher of Gnomenclature at Gnome Countryside. This 15-acre woodland paradise—located off a gravel back lane in a hilly section of Lancaster County, Pennsylvania—is his creation, salvation and love.

It was a rainy spring afternoon outside the town of Kirkwood when we sat inside the Humphreys' 200-year-old, log-and-stone home. The large dining room windows overlooked the picturesque stream and valley below. In an adjacent room, two large bullfrogs burped in low tones as they sat on flat rocks beside the indoor pond, complete with swimming fish.

Richard talked with ease about the little people who have become his specialty during the last quarter century. Listening to him discuss the habits, customs and magic of his unseen friends, it's hard to not believe there must be some gnome genes within him somewhere.

Richard's attire certainly explains why he often is called the "Gnome Man" or "Gnome Guy." A red cap, complete with dangling tassels, covers the top and sides of his head.

"This was made for me by a friend who actually spun the wool herself," he said, patting the top of the cap. "The four colored tassels represent the elements—brown for soil, blue for water, red for fire and white for air."

Around his neck hangs a crow call, which he said he uses to get the attention of visitors as they roam his private gnome sanctuary. Austrian-style lederhosen and heavy hiking boots complete his standard performance attire.

A former art teacher, Richard said that severe diabetes caused him major health problems in the late 1970s; and, in 1980, he was forced to quit his full-time art teaching job.

Getting Richard to explain how the idea of an educational attraction based on gnomes came about took a little time, since there were a number of experiences and circumstances that contributed to his decision to create Gnome Countryside.

As world travelers, he and Mary, his wife of 36 years, had been in Denmark in 1976 and were introduced to an interesting legend.

"The older folks have a serious belief in their little people, called the 'nisse,'" Richard said. "When we were in Denmark on Christmas Eve, we noticed that the folks we stayed with had set out a bowl of porridge for the nisse. They encourage them to stay around. They consider them a source of good luck.

"When we got up on Christmas Day, the porridge had been eaten," Richard said, smiling. Then

> *Since the opening of what he calls his 'environmental and sensory learning experience for the young and young of heart,' about 120,000 visitors have traveled the half-mile series of trails.*

holding up a hand, he added, "Now, they also had several cats in the house. So I'm not saying we can prove the nisse paid a visit. But," he laughed at the memory, "I remember that all of us big people had such fun imagining what may have happened during that night."

While teaching art in the classroom, Richard said he made an important discovery that would affect his future.

"I knew," he said, "that children love two things. They love being outside and they are captivated with the idea of little people. I decided to use the idea of elves as a motivational technique in teaching, since I had read that the idea of little people stimulated children's imaginations."

In 1980, the combination of these two experiences—and his health related limitations—in a way directed him to base his future on the success of Gnome Countryside.

"About 95 percent of my friends told me I was crazy," Richard recalled. "My half-brother told me I

was off the wall. But I knew from my experiences working with children that it would work."

Since the opening of what he calls his "environmental and sensory learning experience for the young and young of heart," about 120,000 visitors have traveled the half-mile series of trails, paused near the talking rocks, been entertained in the amphitheater and, in more than a few cases, thought they've caught a glimpse of a gnome.

A visit to the countryside begins with orientation in the Gnomery, a rustic stone building where "Mr. Rich," as caretaker of his very own gnome village, uses storytelling and singing to teach about the importance of being thoughtful stewards of the environment and share facts and figures about gnomes.

For example, did you know that:

· Little people are believed to exist in nearly every county in the world,

· Gnome mothers always have twins—a boy and a girl,

· Boy gnomes wear red hats and girl gnomes where green hats,

· Gnome hats are pointed at the top so that falling acorns and walnuts will slide down the sides and not clunk the wearer on the head. and

· There are important words, like Gnomenclature and Gnomework.

Following the introduction, "Mr. Rich," as Richard is known during the tour, leads each of the visiting groups through the trail, reinforcing much of his welcoming information and adding new lessons and

The Gnome Man greets visitors with stories and songs in The Gnomery, before he leads them to the Troll Bridge and along the trails of Gnome Countryside.

lore with examples and stories that he shares along the way.

After taking me for a stroll along the mulched trail, Richard paused in the valley beside a flowing creek. He looked up at a formation of jagged rocks, paused and said, "I love this place. I had a couple of very spiritual people tell me there's a lot of energy here, physical and spiritual energy. And if you think of the idea of children looking for signs of the little people out here everywhere, natural stimulation for their imaginations to flourish exists everywhere."

Richard said reporter Jim Ruth put the trail on the map with an article he wrote in a Lancaster paper. "I had a lot of schools call after that. Then, when the story was picked up by the Associated Press, I got calls from around the county."

While school busses deliver a steady flow of school-age visitors, Gnome Countryside has also hosted groups representing churches, scout troops, colleges and even Elderhostels. Families also get together and arrange to visit Richard's woodland wonderland—and over the years there have been many repeat customers who are eager to pass their wonderful experience on to a new generation of gnome seekers.

"I had a first grade teacher here on Thursday," Richard said. "She told me she was here as a first grader and had brought her class with her. I also had a mother who had been to the trail as a first grader bring her daughter, and I told her I am looking forward to leading her granddaughter through the trail one day.

"I've had one child," Richard said, smiling and shaking his head, "who's come back here eight times, between visits with his school and family and scouts. I asked him if he really wanted to come, and he told me he loves it. I think if I got sick he could finish the program for me."

Learning about gnomes is something Richard takes seriously. He said much of his information was taken from the popular book,

entitled *Gnomes*, written by Wil Huygen and illustrated by Rien Poortvliet. Richard and Mary also learned a lot in 1995, while attending the International Gnome Conference in New Zealand.

"Did you know," Richard asked, "that in Iceland they diverted a major road to avoid angering the little people, who are believed to inhabit that area?"

I shook my head, indicating "No."

"I think that's fascinating," Richard said. He also mentioned that through his gnome world he's met a number of wonderful and interesting people. One man delivered several gnome homes, made out of paulownia wood.

"They were absolutely wonderful," Richard said, "and the man told me that he 'Got direct instructions on how to make these from the gnomes. And they don't look anything like they do in the gnome

Vincent Van Gnome watches visitors enter into Gnome Countryside.

books.' You run across a few firm believers over the years," Richard added.

After all his years on the trail and research on the little people, it might seem a bit disappointing to hear that Richard has never actually seen a gnome. But he doesn't seem affected by the lack of gnome proof at all.

One seems to sense that it's the search and the wonder and the magic and the dreams that are more important to the Gnome Man.

Throughout the property are Richard's "talking rocks," pieces of stone engraved with such words as "Joy," "Love," "Hope" and "Dream."

He uses them to teach his gnome trail travelers that there is more to life than the things you can hold in your hand or taste or smell.

As the group pauses at the Dream Rock he usually makes these comments:

Gnome Finders are the ultimate tool for locating shy little people.

"Now boys and girls, I hope each of you is a dreamer and a doer. You see, about 23 years ago, I had a dream that I would have this trail, and that I could walk through it with children and share stories of gnomes and have some simple fun in an outdoor environment. And because of that dream, we all had a good time here today."

Pausing, Richard explained what he believes is the trail's excellent usefulness in teaching. "That's the beauty of it, when you're talking about gnomes, you can work anything into it."

One of his most important messages is that "For hundreds of years we understand that gnomes have been the caretakers of planet Earth. We hope that you would be a caretaker of the forest."

It's obvious that Richard loves his work and his life. And although he must monitor his blood sugar constantly, he has his eye set on a long and productive stewardship of Gnome Countryside. "You've got to take care of yourself," he said. "My goal is to live to be 104, and this trail keeps me going. And, I love what I do."

Oh, there's much more to share, such as the carving of the little one-eared statuette, appropriately named Vincent Van Gnome; the chanting through the bamboo arch; the Gnome Finder goggles; the Troll Bridge and Gnome Niagara; a message from Jerome the Gnome left in an old wasp hive; and the evil man who stole gold from the end of the rainbow. But you can experience all this yourself during your visit to Gnome Countryside.

And when you leave this 15-acre magic haven, like many other visitors you probably will have a few lingering doubts, doubts about your earlier belief that gnomes are imaginary and make believe.

You'll remember that beneath that red cap there was a twinkle in the Gnome Man's eyes. And behind that thick white mustache there was always a sly, secretive smile.

And why did he mention, with a knowing

glance, that 19 years ago his wife, Mary, had twins—a boy, Kesse, and a girl, Kourtney? (Didn't he also say that gnome mothers always give birth to twins, a girl and a boy?) But that's just a coincidence. Isn't it?

Plus, he suggested that you take the wooden Gnome Gnickle and make a wish that something good would happen to someone else—not to yourself. Doesn't that sounds like something only a real-life gnome would do?

No. All this speculation is just a waste of time. After all, there aren't really gnomes . . . are there?

"I'm sort of looked at like a crazy guy," the Gnome Man called out as he waved good-bye from the Gnomery door, "but that's okay with me. You've got to have a few crazy people in this world."

Regina and Ken Brown, in front of their historic home in Smyrna, Delaware

Ken Brown

Smyrna, Delaware

Collecting Delaware

Walking through the front door of Ken Brown's three-story, brick home on a main thoroughfare in historic Smyrna, Delaware, is like passing through a portal that leads the visitor back in time—to an age when workers left their individual mark and talent on everything from furniture and glassware to artwork and eating utensils.

The home of Ken and Regina Brown is a living monument, a personal museum that he, as a collector, has created over time as a tribute to First State artisans, artists and builders.

No mass-produced furniture detracts from the essence of previous centuries that permeates the atmosphere of the Brown residence. Not one aluminum framed print decorates its plaster walls; neither does discount house, going-out-of-business-sale carpeting cover the original, 19th-century polished pinewood floors.

Passing through rooms and hallways or glancing down corridors and alcoves, you realize that this home is a reflection of the residents' personal commitment to preserve the very best of Delaware's historic past.

Now 71, Ken said he was born in a suburb of Smyrna. "I always say," he recalled, smiling, "I was born in Duck Creek, but I moved to Smyrna as soon as I heard about it."

He received his first collectible in 1950, when he was 19. That was when Ken's grandfather gave him an E. A. Prescott, .38 caliber rimfire pistol manufactured in 1860. His grandfather told Ken the Civil War era pistol was used by an ancestor who had fought with the Confederates.

Because of the history associated with the weapon, Ken said he got interested in that particular piece and soon developed a wider interest in collecting firearms.

Over the years, he amassed a large collection of various Colt pocket pistols, particularly those built from 1849-1860. Eventually, he moved to New Castle and began trading his guns for antiques that would furnish his and his wife's historic home.

While visiting Williamsburg in 1956, Ken saw a chest of drawers reproduction selling for $650. Soon afterwards, he came home and met an antique dealer who was offering a period piece for about half that price.

"I bought it!" he said, "My wife and I decided that we needed furniture, so we would collect antiques. Then," he paused and laughed, "the bank got to know me very well. I would borrow money for six or nine months and pay it off. Then I went to another dealer, and there was a fellow there named Charles G. Dorman. He wrote a book on *Delaware Cabinetmakers and Allied Artisans*. Eventually, many things in this house I bought from Charlie Dorman. He was a curator for Independence National Park in Philadelphia."

Ken said it was a fortuitous meeting, and he learned much from his relationship with Dorman over the years. Being a curious person, Ken said the best way to learn about pieces is to handle them, to examine them closely and to ask a lot of questions.

From his early collecting days to the present, he admitted he has amassed an immense amount of knowledge. So much so, that today he is involved in vetting, which is the process of having knowledgeable persons inspect or give opinions about what antique dealers in shows are offering for sale.

"I vet the metals for the Delaware Antique Show for Winterthur Museum," Ken said. "We have life or death decision making on something. We say, 'Yes. It's authentic. No. It's not. Take it out of the booth.' And

then we can say, 'This was really made in 1890, not 1780. Retag it!' So I guess I think I know my silver. I have had discussions with dealers, and I have sometimes prevailed over what they think it is that they have."

Leaving out license plates and matchcovers, Ken's interest in Delaware-made items is far reaching, involving money, books, furniture, glassware, dinnerware, textiles, needlepoint samplers and art.

"I have collections of collections," he said. Pointing to a mantle shelf in his library, he added, "These snuff bottles were packed at the snuff mill in Yorklyn, Delaware."

Quickly leaving his chair, Ken moved across the room and shouted, "You're going to get a wealth of useless information," then returned and handed me what looked like a candle wrapped in cellophane.

As I examined the piece, he explained, "This was the early way they wrapped snuff, in a turkey gullet."

"What's a turkey gullet?" I asked.

"Intestines. This is the way they first sold snuff in the 1780s."

Ken said one of his primary interests is in securing the signatures of Delaware's governors.

"I probably need 50," he said. "I have about 18. Some of them are difficult to find. Roger Martin is the reason I started collecting governors' signatures. We were at a Dover meeting and I purchased a copy of Roger's book, *A History of Delaware Through Its Governors, 1776-1984*. As I was talking to him, he said, 'You know, some of those signatures are quite rare.' So that piqued my curiosity."

Explaining that he has found Delaware pieces in such far away places as Los Angeles and Florida, he acknowledged he's moved into the modern age, securing some items through Internet on-line auctions with assistance from his wife, Regina.

Throughout our conversation, the connection between each object and history was apparent. With every piece Ken shared an associated story, whether it was about the craft in general and its creator or the treasured item in particular.

While speaking with Ken, I learned that the small state of Delaware had more than 50 working silversmiths in the 19th century—more than similar artisans operating in Kentucky or in South Carolina at the same time. Despite prohibitions from the Crown, I discovered that Delaware—along with the other colonies—issued paper money. But the First State did not produce coinage, as was minted in New Jersey, New Hampshire, New York and Massachusetts.

Ken explained that because of Delaware's small size some Delaware-made items are perceived to be rare. But, he stressed, this is not always the case. However, this is an ongoing argument he has with dealers around the country, some of whom charge inflated prices for anything old that is believed to have been made in Delaware.

What about Delaware books?

"I wouldn't call myself a book collector. I'm a knowledge collector," Ken said. "I'm seeking information, that's why I have these books. I have interest, to a degree, in publications. I have the important editions. There is also this same number of books on my third floor landing that I don't have space for. In collecting books and furniture, you have to take space into consideration, most certainly."

Ken said he attends a large number of Delaware-related auctions throughout the state. He admitted that there are people who have much more knowledge about certain Delaware objects—such as license plates and salt and pepper sets. But in areas where he has extensive experience, he has seen people who will spend five times more than certain items are worth.

"Unfortunately, they have no idea of the value," he said. "They will pay horrendous amounts for certain items that are far above their value. But, apparently, money was not a problem for some of them. There's this romance with certain Delaware items, and people start to collect them."

The sad thing, Ken said, is when he deals with people that have paid inflated amounts for certain collections and then later try to recoup their investment.

"They are confronted with the fact that they have

paid far above the object's or a collection's worth," he said. "It's a shame."

Since he's amassed several years of experience, I asked Ken what advice he would offer collectors.

Without hesitation, he replied, "Read the book first. And then handle the objects, ask lots of questions. Go slow, and buy from trusted dealers. If it looks too good to be true, it probably is not true. You've got to know what you're buying, and there are lots of people who don't."

When people bid without enough background knowledge, their actions also can have an unpleasant effect upon established dealers and collectors.

At a Smyrna auction, Ken said he and Regina had noticed a 1790-era cream pot that was scheduled for sale. He estimated its value at from $2,500 to $3,000. When it came up for sale, the dealers dropped out at $2,000. It eventually sold for $4,600.

"The auctioneer ended up doing a great job for the estate," Ken said, referring to the inflated price that the auction house was able to secure for the estate that had owned the item.

Another unique thing about collecting is the attachment that some people develop with the items they find, bid upon and secure.

"Over the years, I've acquired thousands of items. But I have regretted everything I've ever sold or traded," Ken said. "Absolutely. That's because I've bought something because I was interested in it. And I have let it go because of economic necessity or to get something better or due to lack of interest in an item—at that particular time. Now, I just don't dispose of things. That's not to say I wouldn't trade for something I was really interested in."

As we walked through the first floor of the Brown's home, looking for the best location to take his picture, we passed by two gold-framed, oil portraits of Enoch and Anne Spruance, painted by an unknown artist, possibly Bass Otis, in 1825; I touched a Windsor chair, crafted in the 1830s by Jared Chestnut of Wilmington; I took a seat in a piece of furniture, made by W. Cox of New Castle nearly two centuries ago; I viewed a rare lithograph of a Red Lion Camp Meeting and gazed at a watercolor by Lydia Burton of Lewes, created in 1795; I touched a Delaware State platter, made in 1820 by the Stafforshire Pottery in England; I lifted a needlepoint Wilmington Academy sampler, stitched in 1813; and I listened to the delicate chimes of a tall case clock, made in about 1810 by the hands of Jacob Wright of Sunbury, Pa.

At that moment, when each piece was touched, I could sense a connection with the artist, a closeness with the craftsman or painter who had worked or lived in Delaware centuries ago. Certainly, the experience is another intangible benefit of collecting.

Looking across his long formal parlor, Ken shared an adage he had once heard. "Henry F. du Pont said, 'When you're collecting, you either have it or you don't.' He was referring to the money to secure the item and the ability to select pieces properly.

"I've paid dearly for some items, but I have them. Eventually, the market will catch up with what I paid. And I'm sure some people say, 'Look at that damn fool.' But when I want something, I get it."

Regina and Ken enjoying tea in their Colonial-era dining room

Wally Jones

Elkton, Maryland

Bill Lowe

Lewes, Delaware

A Pair of River Pilots

In the closing days of the 20th century, many traditional jobs have been relegated to faded pictures in old family photograph albums and newspaper clippings and images in the files of historical society archives. High technology and changing lifestyles have combined to create new occupations that reflect a modern, mobile, sophisticated age.

But, if you know where to look, you can still find people in more traditional jobs that have survived the passage of time. Among the region's workers who can give us a glimpse of the past are members of the more than 100-year-old association representing the Pilots of the Bay and River Delaware.

Between them, Bill Lowe and Wally Jones—two of the organization's members—have spent nearly 100 years guiding ships up and down the Delaware River. Their recollections show how this centuries-old occupation has changed and how much it has remained the same.

Bill has lived in Lewes, Delaware, nearly all of his life. His home is within walking distance of the Delaware Bay where he spends much of his time. Since colonial times, he said, this small seaport town where the Atlantic Ocean meets the Delaware Bay has been known as the East Coast home of a large number of the region's river guides.

A Delaware River pilot can be found in Lowe's family tree for 10 generations, beginning with John Maull, who guided wooden boats and iron men up and down the busy East Coast waterway. That ancestor on Lowe's mother's side began working the river in the 1750s, before the Revolutionary War. And Lowe's son, William III, currently is piloting the river and bay, continuing the family tradition into the next generation.

It was while he was in Lewes High School, in 1952 at the age of 17, that Bill signed on as an apprentice. For $5 a month, he chipped paint, did assorted chores, assisted the working pilots and learned the basics of seamanship from the bottom up.

In 1956, he piloted his first ship, and he remembers that event vividly.

"It was June 1, 1956," Bill recalled. "It was a World War II Liberty Ship, the *Elna*. I took it to Philadelphia. I think every pilot remembers his first solo ship. It was like graduating from the University of Delaware, or getting your first job."

Wally's piloting career started with his apprenticeship in 1958. A resident of Elkton, Maryland, he recently retired after 40 years working the river. Like many pilots, he lives some distance from the mouth of the Delaware Bay,

"I was 17," Wally remembered. "My father was a deep sea captain for ARCO, which was then Atlantic Refining. When he would come in from a foreign port, he would have to take a pilot. Through the years, he

> *'The biggest one I've ever been on is 1,200 feet long. It was a tanker. I've been on all kinds of military ships—destroyers, submarines, PT boats, pretty much everything else. Once, I came up the Delaware with the Navy SEALS. That was an experience. I think we made record time.'*
>
> —*Wally Jones*

met some of the pilots and became friendly. One of them offered that, when I came of age, if I wanted to become a pilot he would sponsor me. In 1958, I graduated from Valley Forge Military Academy in June and started on the boat in August. But I always wanted to do it. My father took me and my mother down to visit the pilot boat in Lewes. I must have been about 12, and I was very impressed by it. "

Wally's apprenticeship lasted four years. At that time, he said, the apprentices ran the launches—smaller boats, about 48 feet—that would take the pilots to and from the ships, and they maintained the large pilot boat. In the late '50s, it was an old Coast Guard icebreaker that served as a station off Lewes.

"The pilots would sleep on there in between ships," Wally said. "We ran it in the bay, and it was always under way. They don't do that any longer. When I began, there were wooden launches. Now they're all metal. They had just begun to start using the metal boats when I got there. After you finished the apprenticeship, you became a licensed pilot. "

Wally explained that the license is specifically for the Delaware River. The pilots are responsible for guiding shipping from the mouth of the Delaware Bay about 130 miles—as far north as Morrisville, at a U. S. Steel plant, in Trenton. In the south, there's an imaginary line between Lewes, Delaware, and Cape May, New Jersey, that separates international from inland waters. While Wally didn't take ships through the Chesapeake and Delaware Canal, many of the other pilots do, since the Delaware Bay pilots are responsible for guiding vessels through the eastern portion of the canal.

Bill Lowe, looking out at the Delaware Bay from the walkway near the top of the Maritime Exchange Tower in Cape Henlopen State Park.

"They change at Chesapeake City, near Schaefer's Canal House," Wally said. "You see the small boats go out of Schaefer's, that's what they're doing. The Baltimore pilots pick it up from there. Each port has its own pilots' association.

"I love it," Wally said. "I enjoy handling ships, and I enjoy meeting the people from all over the world. It's like being a world traveler but never leaving home. "

The business of guiding ships never stops and, for river pilots, holidays don't exist. Except for a brief stall during severe weather conditions, pilots guide incoming and outgoing ships 365 days a year, 24 hours a day.

"I was on duty one Christmas Day," Bill recalled, "working the tower at Cape Henlopen. I was listening to the radio and this DJ was talking about how bad it was that he had to work and wondered if anyone out there was listening to him. I called him up and said, 'A lot of people have to work on holidays, the police and hospital personnel.' And I wanted to let him know that the pilot association was at work in the pilot station doing its part. "

When ships arrive from the ocean, the pilots have to be ready to be taken out to sea on a craft that is similar to a large speedboat. When they reach the ship in the ocean, the smaller boat pulls alongside the moving ship. The pilot climbs a dangling rope ladder and boards the moving vessel.

"Some of them," Wally said, "are only five or six steps and some of them are 40 feet to the main deck. We have a fellow on the launch who puts his foot on the bottom of the rope ladder to steady it. We have very excellent people that run the launches. They're most important. The ships come in, they'll make a lee, to try to swing the ship to keep all the weather on the opposite side from the ladder, so it's as smooth as possible.

"Once on the main deck, the pilot is escorted directly to the bridge and takes control. We're taken to the bridge where we serve as advisers. The captain and I exchange information. He'll tell me the characteristics of the ship, if there are any problems. I'll tell him weather and tide conditions, whatever else he needs to know. Then I give the commands."

"Our office is open every day of the year," Bill said, referring to personnel who work at the pilot association's Philadelphia office and dispatch site, and the other members who are stationed in Lewes to communicate with and board and guide incoming ships. The association's pilots also board outgoing ships at the Delaware River's northern ports—such as Philadelphia, Camden, Wilmington and Delaware City—to guide the vessels out to sea.

In his Lewes home, surrounded by fading documents and family artifacts reflecting 10 generations and hundreds of years working the water, Bill often made reference to the past.

The Maritime Exchange Tower, where the Pilots of the Bay and River Delaware monitor ship traffic, originally was a World War II fire control tower.

An avid historian, he explained how American Indians originally guided white settlers' ships up the Delaware River. He speaks of Lewes' importance to shipping before the days of electronic communication, and he tells of the pilots' important role in commerce and war.

During 1998, Bill said it had been 46 years since he signed on as an apprentice. As an aside, the

knowledgeable navigator of the waters admitted that one thing he doesn't like to do is travel.

"I like Delaware," he said. "I like to explore strange places. But, this job enables me to meet people from all over the world. I've been on British ships, Italian ships, Korean ships. I have met people from all over the world. I try their food and learn how they are different. In a few hours on the river, I get a sense of their culture, then a few hours later I'm back home."

One of the concerns of piloting—and it happens occasionally—is not being able to get off a ship that is exiting the bay in rough seas. When the smaller craft that delivers and picks up pilots has not been able to reach a departing ship, weeks later, the pilot has ended up in a foreign country, and some of them are not five-star tourist destinations.

"I came very close to being carried away," Bill said. "It was New Year's Eve, and I was setting out of Delaware City. The ship was headed for Venezuela, and I almost didn't get off. But I made it. Now," he added, laughing, "if I was captive on a passenger ship that would be fun. But you wouldn't want to be taken to Saudi Arabia on a tanker to get crude oil. We've had to send passports and documents to pilots when that happens."

Wally laughed, recalling a similar incident. "I almost got carried off last December. I was on a Finnish paper ship. I thought they were going to a place in Canada that I never heard of. But I ended up getting off. I had a couple seconds of a calm spot and I scampered down and got off. Later, I discov-

ered that it wasn't Canada they were going to, it was the east coast of Finland. That's why I had never heard of it before. That was close to Christmas. I would not have been a happy camper."

Bill has guided everything from tugboats pulling mammoth barges and fruit ships to gleaming passenger liners and the battleship *USS New Jersey*.

When he started in the mid-1950s, large ships were about 550 feet long and less than 100 feet wide. Today, Very Large Crude Carriers (VLCCs) weigh 270,000 tons and are 1,100 feet in length and 179 feet wide. These metal monsters that are several stories high can carry 10 times the capacity that they did years ago. And while technology and navigational advances—including computers and satellite imagery—have aided the pilots' ability to know exact locations, the tremendous growth

'This is like any job, when it's working well its very satisfying and when it's not it's very frightening. On the water, it can be 90 percent routine and 10 percent sheer terror.'

—Bill Lowe

of the ships has not made the job any easier. In fact, the immense increase in size and load capability have reduced the margin of human and mechanical error.

Bill said the cargo that leaves and enters the Delaware River is a reflection of the changes in the economy and a response to the needs and wants of the consumer. Years ago, coal and grain were exported from Philadelphia. Today, those commodities are no longer major products and rarely travel the river.

Currently, Wilmington is regarded as a major East Coast import site of bananas, and ships filled with automobiles make regular stops at the northern Delaware port.

Of course, millions of barrels of crude oil continue to be delivered to refineries that stretch from Delaware City to Pennsylvania. Bill stressed that with the massive amount of oil traveling the Delaware River and Bay, the pilots boast an excellent record with very few accidents or spills.

"The biggest one I've ever been on is 1,200 feet long," Wally said. "It was a tanker. I've been on all kinds of military ships—destroyers, submarines, PT boats, pretty much everything else. Once, I came up the Delaware with the Navy SEALS. That was an experience," he said, smiling. "I think we made record time. In fact, the only type of military ship I haven't been on is an aircraft carrier."

Wally explained that there's a channel through which pilots lead the mamouth ships. While the pathway doesn't shift, he explained, it's being dredged all the time.

"There are areas that will, what they call, 'silt,'" he said. "From where the channel starts in the bay it's 1,000 feet wide at a depth of 40 feet. It's what we call project depth—that's 40 feet at low water. At high water you have about 45, 46 feet, depending upon the wind. The wind has a lot of effect upon the waters in the river. When you get up around Bombay Hook, it narrows to around 800 feet. Up around the harbor in Philadelphia there's a deep channel that's 400 feet. The ships are about 130 feet wide. It's enough space.

"But the job's never routine," Wally added. "Each ship is different. Each ship has its own characteristics. The weather's never the same. Traffic conditions are never the same. Some day you can take a ship up the river and never see another ship, and some days there are ships everywhere. In the summer, you have to be aware of recreational boaters. They're all over the river and bay, and often they don't see you or aren't aware that they should look out for you."

While a car drive from Lewes to Philadelphia can take about two-and-a-half hours, a trip up the Delaware River channel on a 1,000-foot-long tanker loaded with crude oil is a lot longer.

"How long it takes depends on the ship," Wally said. "It could be six hours or nine hours. It depends on how fast the ship is and, to a degree, weather conditions. Weather can make a six-hour trip a long six hours. There are times we've had ice in the bay. And a few times it's been bad enough to stop traffic. There comes a point that you can't do it, that it's just too dangerous to try and board ship. But that doesn't happen often. I can remember, maybe, three or four times we've gone off station since I've been there, that means not working other ships. It's usually rough but doable."

After nearly a half-century on the water, Bill's conversation and tone reflects definite pride and satisfaction. His ancestors navigated the same waterway where he has spent his entire working life. He added with pride that his son, William III, chose freely and without pressure to extend an honorable family tradition.

"If you don't enjoy your job," Bill said, "it doesn't matter how much money you receive. My son feels the same way. But, this is like any job, when it's working well its very satisfying and when it's not it's very frightening. On the water, it can be 90 percent routine and 10 percent sheer terror. When things happen, you have to make decisions. Sometimes, you have to decide whether you should quit or keep going."

Wally talked about some of the changes he's seen over the last four decades. They range from new apprentices with college degrees and females in the ranks to the latest high-tech equipment.

"About two years ago," he said, "we added the DGPS, it's part of the Global Positioning Satellite System. It's incredible. It's a laptop with an antenna. We each have one, and when we get on board we put up the antenna. It has a receiver and converter. It will allow me to position myself within one meter. Initially, I humbugged it, and I have since eaten every word. It's an incredible machine and it's incredibly accurate. But, you have to keep in mind that it's an aide. There's a disclaimer on the computer that more or less says, 'Don't forget to look out the window.' When the systems fail, you still have to be able to do it the old way."

Toward the end of our meeting, Bill produced a diary that had been kept by his grandfather, John E. Maull. He opened the worn, leather book and pointed to script handwriting that listed all the ships Lowe's ancestor had piloted from 1901-1920. During a career that spanned 18 years and 7 months, Bill's grandfather worked on 795 ships.

In the same time period, Bill Lowe's records indicate that he had worked 3,725 ships, and to date his number has reached more than 6,000.

"That doesn't mean they spent less time working," Bill explained of the early pilots. "It's just that there was less communication in those days. They would keep 10 pilots out on the pilot boat, waiting for ships to appear.

"But, times have changed. The old pilots spent a lot of time out there sitting and eating. That's why when you see their pictures, they look like this," he said, smiling and forming the shape of a pear with his hands. "They weren't on any type of health oriented diet. Those cooks on the pilot boats were feeding them wonderfully. One of the things that changed when we decided to do away with the pilot boats and come ashore to the pilot station was also to do away with the cooks."

One gets the impression that the passing of the old cooks is one of the things that older pilots, like Bill and Wally, miss.

Author's note: Bill Lowe passed away on June 8, 2002. This story is based on interviews conducted with Mr. Lowe and Wally Jones in 1998 and 2000.

George Kreigh

Lincoln, Delaware

License Plate Man

Talk about collecting in Delaware and someone always seems to mention "license
plates. " According to those in the know,
First Staters are absolutely crazy about securing a "low
numbered" vehicle tag. Over the years, for some it
has become the ultimate status symbol.

According to an article entitled "Delaware
License Plates Not Just Ordinary Tags" that appeared
in the September 1998 issue of *Southern Delaware
Magazine*, "A few years ago at an auction in the
Rehoboth Beach Convention Center, several hundred people watched as bidding for a single digit tag
rose to $185,000. " And in the *Automobile License
Plate Collectors Association* (ALPCA) *Newsletter*, a
publication for serious plate collectors, a short story
by Richard E. Dragon noted that a 1986 Trans Am
sold in 1989 for $70,000, "only because attached to
the back of the car was Delaware registration number
79. "

While these low-numbered treasures are always
in demand, there also are plate hunters whose aim is
more basic—to increase the number of plates in their
collections. Among the best known auto plate collectors in the Diamond State is George Kreigh, 71, of
Lincoln, Delaware.

I first met George at Potters' Hickory Ridge
Steam Show outside Milford, Delaware. His colorful
display of hundreds of license plates, arranged on
large sheets of interlocking plywood, attracted a large
number of interested observers.

Months later, in the basement of his Sussex
County home, standing near special racks holding
more than 6,000 license plates, George explained

that the annual June event at Hickory Ridge was the
only place he continued to display portions of his huge
collection.

"I'm getting older now, " George said, adding
that it takes a lot of energy and effort to lug around
his heavy displays.

Despite his age, the U. S. Navy veteran keeps an
active schedule, continuing the community service
that he's been involved in throughout his life. He's a
life member of the Farmington Volunteer Fire
Company and past president of the Delaware State
Fire Police. Retired from the DuPont Company since
1985, he keeps busy delivering parts for an auto deal-
ership and serving as chaplain of the Farmington Fire
Company.

With such a busy schedule, he said his collection
provides an opportunity for him to relax and occasionally wonder about the stories behind some of his
metal plates.

George said he can still recall the exact moment
that he decided to get into the hobby that has
demanded many hours of attention and provided him
with immense satisfaction.

He was watching TV coverage of the 1969
Apollo 11 moon landing when he saw a number of
cars passing by on the television screen and, for some
reason, he noticed their license plates.

"I don't know why, exactly, " George said, "but I
wanted to have something to do. Then I thought it
would be interesting to collect license plates from
around the country. "

After securing a mailing list with the addresses of
motor vehicle offices around the U. S. , and making

trips to area salvage yards, he started a hobby that has kept him busy for more than 30 years.

"When I started," George said, "I could get them off wrecks in junk yards and they would charge you about $4 for a stack of 10 to 15 tags. Today, you'll pay $5 to $10 each."

Selecting a few handfuls of his flat metal treasures—that include a wide variety of tags for such motorized vehicles as taxis, limousines, cars, school buses, antique and diplomatic vehicles, campers, trucks and state-owned transports—George glances at each and speaks effortlessly. His voice seems both humble and self-assured, as he shares appropriate portions of the wealth of knowledge he has gained during the last three decades.

Most tags are 6 inches high by 12 inches wide.

For taxis, depending upon the state, there are numerous designations stamped or printed on the tags. In New York it's "livery"; in Maryland and Louisiana it's "hire"; in Virginia, a large "H"; in Tennessee, it's "taxi"; and this list goes on.

Offering samples of automobile plates from different states, George pointed out the artwork and symbols.

Wyoming's cowboy on the bucking bronco, he said, goes clear back to 1936, and this makes it one of the earliest plates with a symbol that, interestingly, is still being used. Then there's Maine's lobster, Colorado's mountains, the wheat of Kansas, the Aztec symbol in New Mexico. Of course he's got 45 more states to share.

Flipping through another stack, George showed off his "Bicentennial" plates, which many states offered as a special edition in 1976. From the Massachusetts Minuteman to Pennsylvania's Liberty Bell, George recognized them all and offered a quick comment about several.

Then there was the story about Delaware's license plates:

· How in 1905, the first year vehicles were registered, and owners made their own tags out of leather and metal house-number numerals.

· That the very first Delaware plate was issued in 1909. (George's Delaware collection goes from 1910 to the present.).

· That the First State plate progressed through leather, porcelain, heavy metal, porcelain, stainless steel and aluminum.

· How Delaware is the only state that has a flat plate with numbers painted onto the surface. All other states have numbers pressed into their license tags.

George holds a Maine plate from the death car in Kittery, Maine.

George admits that he's slowed up recently, isn't out collecting as much. But he continues to trade with other collectors throughout the country and around the world.

"I was always interested in history," he said, running the tips of his fingers across the racks of several state plates. "You can tell about a place from the pictures and artwork on their license plates. I got a Maine one up there I have to show you.

It's got something written on the back. Let me find it. "

Then pulling a dark, slightly charred piece of rectangular metal from the Maine rack, he passed it to me and said, "Read the back. "

The handwritten script stated: "The death car. Grace's Ford coupe that killed Mrs. Brown in Kittery, Maine, in 1918. "

"It came off a Model T in 1918," George said. "It's something to have the tag that came off the car, and you can see where the metal was scorched from the fire. Yep. There's a lot of history in these plates. "

As we were summarizing his thoughts, George recalled a special moment that occurred one day when his nephew stopped by and handed the collector a number 13 Delaware POW tag. The license plate had belonged to George's brother, who was an ex-prisoner of war. When his brother had died, the plate was lost for a period of time. George's nephew found it and gave it to his uncle.

"It just got to me," George said. "I wondered what happened to it. That meant a whole lot, that that boy would come over and give it to me. "

Joe Daddiego

New Providence, Pennsylvania

Blacksmith & Son

To most drivers, the message on the black, hand-lettered sign poking out from the high grass beside Pennsy Road in Lancaster County, Pennsylvania, tells it all: Amish buggy drivers should keep clopping on by and search for a furrier, who works with horseshoes; but tourists should pull onto the gravel drive and stop to examine the fine sculpted ironworks shaped in the old wooden workshop.

Some visiting browsers, particularly those with a discerning ear and an eye for detail, might realize there is more to the story than the large man with the heavy hammer who sweats over white-hot coals.

When words like Tony Bennett, Monticello, Billy Joel and Haitian drums are sprinkled in the conversation, it becomes automatic, almost required, that the visitor ask the bearded man with the Brooklyn accent what led him to settle along a back road in the middle of nowhere—far from America's largest city, where he grew up and learned his trades. And, of course, they'll also want to hear about his connection with some of the world's most famous recording artists.

We sat in the kitchen of Joe Daddiego's farmhouse, where he lives with his son, Joe, and wife, Ginny. Now 58, the blacksmith grew up in Manhattan. He casually mentioned that he made the wrought iron table at which we were sitting. Using the stem of his pipe, he pointed to the sculptures in the adjacent living room, and at the shelves and racks and the other pieces of furniture and artistic creations that filled the rooms and covered the walls.

"They're all my work," he mentioned, figuring the items would give me an idea of the type of objects that he creates.

It was obvious that he enjoyed talking about his early years, when he learned the family trade from his father. Proudly, Joe stressed, "I'm a fifth generation blacksmith from Italy. But, my son, Joey, who works with me now is the sixth."

Joe Daddiego and his son, Joe, who is carrying on the family trade into a sixth generation

Joe's Italian neighborhood, beneath the Manhattan Bridge, was adjacent to an area that was populated by immigrants from Brazil, Cuba, the Caribbean and South America. In the early 1960s, Joe said he and his father began using their blacksmithing skills to make cow bells and keys and equipment for the Latin and African musicians in lower Manhattan.

"I was about 11 at the time," he recalled, "and I fell in love with the music and the romance associated with the instruments. Soon, I was learning to play the Spanish and Portuguese rhythms."

After school and during the weekends, Joe said he worked with his father in the shop, creating ornamental ironwork for some upscale customers. "We didn't do much standard work," Joe said. "Our specialty was creating new pieces in the neo-European and contemporary design. Free form, you would call it. At that time, blacksmiths were in demand and people wanted to have fancy, one-of-a-kind creations."

Their customers included Dom DeLuise and Mayor Ed Koch.

"We made him [Koch] a 10-foot length of gate," Joe said. "It took a month to finish because there was so much detail to do."

During that period of time, there was a steady demand for exquisitely fabricated gates, wall hangings, frames, trellises, furniture, fireplace accessories and lighting fixtures, Joe said. In his spare time, Joe learned to speak Spanish and became a proficient drummer. At nights, he began playing with some of the best Latin bands in the city.

"My love," he said, "was in the real Afro-Cuban and Brazilian music. Eventually, I was doing recording dates for TV commercials and records. I played in bands and worked with a number of stars, including Tony Bennett, Aretha Franklin, Jose Feliciano and Ritchie Havens. This was all in New York, in the recording studio and for live performances. I was working with a number of the bands in the Latin circuit. Almost every weekend I would go upstate and play in the Catskills. I'd blacksmith in the day and perform at night. I could take off now and then, because I was working for my father and it was his business."

Joe's wife, Ginny, who is the heart of the current business in New Providence, suggested that Joe share the story about his encounter with Billy Joel.

Laughing at the memory, Joe explained that he had been booked to travel to a very large estate on Long Island to play background drums on a demo recording. The owner of the property, Joe was told, was well off and had a recording studio in his home.

In front of their shop, the son and father blacksmiths display a fence they created.

"It was in about 1983," Joe said. "I was heavy into Latin/Afro/Caribbean music. They needed somebody to play that stuff. I didn't know who Billy Joel was. So, we took a break and I was having a drink with Billy. I told him I worked in the studios a lot and I had seen a lot of people getting shelved. That means they don't shop their music around, just put it aside for tax purposes.

"I told him that I've seen them come and go. Then I said, 'But you have a lot of talent and terrific quality in your voice. You should take your work out there. You can make it.' Then I said, 'And you should listen to me, Billy, because I know what I'm talking about.' "

After politely accepting Joe's advice, the Piano Man invited the blacksmith/musician to take a short walk.

"He brings me into the front entrance of his house," Joe said. "There's a long hall into a sun-room, and on all the walls are platinum and gold records and framed awards for songs he has written. I said, 'I don't believe this! Are all these yours?' And he says, 'Yeah!' Then I said, 'God bless you! But at least I know what I'm talking about!'

"When I got home," Joe said, smiling and shaking his head at the memory, "I told my wife I was with Billy Joel and she started screaming and was upset that I didn't get his autograph."

Eventually, two major changes in New York City affected Joe's livelihood. The first was the decline in the quality of life. Wealthy people began moving out of the city, and this exodus reduced the amount of requests for fine ironwork. Instead of jobs requiring intricate filigree and creativity, Joe and his father began filling orders for window bars and security equipment for commercial and residential buildings. They found this simple, unchallenging drone work unsatisfying.

Also, recording studios began to use digital equipment and recordings of musicians to back up singers. Consequently, the need and opportunities for live musicians were drying up.

After talking to his father, Joe decided he had to make a change. He had visited and worked in Lancaster County and mentioned that he liked the beauty of the area and he thought it had potential.

"My father said New York City was no bargain no more," Joe recalled. "He agreed that I should look for a new place to raise my family."

After spending five years looking for the right location, Joe and Ginny decided that the 17-acre plot in New Providence would fit the bill. In 1988, they moved from the Big Apple, bringing their 17-year-old daughter, Samantha, and 10-year-old son, Joey.

Ginny recalled that the first night they stayed in their 19th-century farmhouse, Samantha "looked at how black it was outside and asked what time the street lights go on." The teenager was amazed that there were no lights or sidewalks, and she was afraid of bears. In fact, she swore that if she saw a trace of a bear, she would be heading back to New York.

Relocating from the city to the country had a dramatic effect on Joe's profession. Instead of crafting imaginative designs for the rich and famous, the man who had repaired a chandelier that hangs in Monticello began forging basic utilitarian pieces—tools, plow blades and tractor parts.

"It was functional," he said, "but I was happy to have the work. I never moved to Pennsy Road to make money. You don't leave New York City to become the best blacksmith in my little corner of Lancaster County. Where I used to do work for the rich, I was now talking to Amish farmers. It was different, but it was a good change."

> *'When I got home, I told my wife I was with Billy Joel, and she started screaming and was upset that I didn't get his autograph.'*
>
> —Joe Daddiego

Pausing, Joe tried to explain the dramatic differences between New York City and his current home of 15 years.

"Unless you make $200,000 a year, no sane person in their right mind would live in New York. They're not bad people, they just have a different sense of priorities. You can leave your house anytime of the day or night and there are 8 million people going to the same place.

"This is heaven! When I explain it to people, they look at me like I'm an alien or something."

Ginny explained that when she went to a local bank to open a checking account, she finished the task and was back home in 15 minutes. But Joe was so shocked when she returned that he wanted to know if the bank had been closed or if there was a robbery and she couldn't get inside.

"In New York," she said, "I would wait in line for one-and-a-half hours just to cash one of Joe's checks. And to open a new account, it takes three to four hours, and I'm not exaggerating."

Jumping in to add another example, Joe said the car, truck and cab horns are non-stop, blaring all day and night.

"If you want to make a million dollars in New York, go into horns and horn repairs. Most people don't know this."

Over the years, Joe's business has expanded and local professionals have discovered his artistic talents. His work is in the homes of doctors, professionals and politicians and he is recommended by interior decorators. His customers come from as far as New York, Maryland and Washington, D.C.

"My wife stood by me," Joe said. "She supported every move I made and she knew we would make it when most people said I wouldn't. Much of our work comes from satisfied customers, by word of mouth."

When asked about the strangest item he ever was asked to build, Joe laughed, recalling the two women who came into his New York workshop one Friday night.

"They said, 'We want a collapsible cage made, and we're going to use it . . .' I stopped them and told them I can make their cage on one condition, that they don't tell me what it's for. That was about the wildest thing I ever made."

Joe acknowledged that a lot of people have some wrong ideas about blacksmithing.

"Most people find my work interesting, but most think I do horseshoes," Joe said. "But furriers do horseshoes. Also, people don't understand the nature and demands of the work.

"When you're doing a 150-foot-long fence involving extensive free hand design, they don't realize the repetitiveness and the time and labor that goes into what's involved with the scrolls and vines. There are the patinas and texture and burning procedures, and the chemicals and lacquers that are needed to accent the highlights. There's a big difference between a fabricator and a blacksmith."

It's obvious that Joe is proud of his creations. During the conversation he pointed out some of the furniture and sculptures he had formed by hand. What he said is rare is finding someone to carry on the tradition and learn the techniques he has been taught.

Offers to take on apprentices have produced very few inquiries. In the rare instances that youngsters

> *'It's very satisfying to be able to work with my father and learn from him. He's worked his whole life for me, and now I get to return the favor. The most important thing my father taught me is how to work, and he also taught me how to learn. Once you learn those things in life, you're set.'*
>
> —*Joey Daddiego*

have sought information, they decided the work was too hard and too demanding.

"This work is my love. But I'm going blind, I have acute glaucoma, but my son, Joe, is taking over more and more of the work. I'm not working as much as I used to. I miss it, but I still get a chance to do some of the artistic work. But the welding, I can't do that anymore."

While walking from the farmhouse to the blacksmith shop, Joe spoke proudly about his 24-year-old son, who enthusiastically chose to carry on the family trade.

"He's very good," the father said. "He's doing things in half the time that it takes me."

An amateur boxer with an interest in physical therapy, the younger blacksmith paused from his work to talk about his profession and the guidance his parents have provided.

"I really enjoy the work a lot," he said. "There's nothing like being able to learn and operate your own business. This is a wonderful opportunity. But I have to stress that my mother is our biggest supporter. She's responsible for everything I've done in my life. She'll also tell us the truth about our work."

Joe said his son started learning the business when he was 8, so he's already gotten 16 years of on-the-job training.

"It's very satisfying to be able to work with my father and learn from him," young Joe said. "He's worked his whole life for me, and now I get to return the favor. The most important thing my father taught me is how to work, and he also taught me how to learn. Once you learn those things in life, you're set."

Author's note: To contact Joe about his work, call him at (717) 786-3076.

Photograph by Jerry Rhodes

Tom Frey

Dagsboro, Delaware

The Root of the Sculptor

Tom Frey, wood turner extraordinaire from Dagsboro, Delaware, is proof of the old adage that it's never too late to start living your dream.

For the 65-year old Ocean View native, the dream has always been to do things with wood that are just a bit different from what others are doing. In Tom's case, the dream had to wait until family and career responsibilities had been met.

What he has done since his retirement as an auto mechanic in 1987, however, is to turn out some of the most elegant and evocative pieces of turned wood in the Delmarva area. Not only are his works highly sought after by local collectors, but his beautifully polished vessels of native wood have found homes in places across America and around the world, including Japan, China, Holland and the British Isles.

Tom's fascination with wood turning began under the guidance of his junior high school wood-shop teacher, Herman Koenig. "In that class, you had to learn how to use all the different tools," Tom recalled. "It was very interesting—I turned out two bowls while I was there."

Following retirement, Tom picked up where he had left off in Herman Koenig's class when he unpacked a lathe from the box in which it had lain for nearly a decade.

"I remembered some unusual stuff that I had seen in pictures over the years," Tom said. "I started doing unusual things with distressed wood—things they tell you not to do until you have had some turning experience."

Although it took a while to master the art of working with the natural edge of the wood, Tom said he eventually moved from working on thicker pieces to the thin-walled creations for which he is recognized by friends and fellow artisans.

"I want to work with unusual wood that has begun to go back to nature," Tom said. "The more it is going in this direction, or the more worm and bug holes it may have the better. That's the stuff I like working with."

Much of the wood is taken from the considerable stacks that sprawl out across Tom's back yard, each labeled to indicate the year it was cut and its type.

Photograph by Jerry Rhodes

Tom's creations are made from a variety of woods. Clockwise, from top right, are pieces created from sugar maple, white oak, honey locust and silver maple.

Friends have helped to build this stockpile by offering him wood they think would be of interest to him.

"I leave most of my wood out in the weather," Tom said, "and once a year I cut an end off to check what's going on inside."

While most of his material is from Delmarva, Tom is always on the lookout for any wood that nature has marked or distressed in an unusual way.

Favorite woods for Tom include maple and magnolia, but he also has a ready stock of cherry, silver maple, oak, plum, sassafras, dogwood and American holly. He also uses persimmon and mesquite, as well as roots from shrubs such as rhododendron, yew, azalea and wild grapevine.

Time and experience, Tom noted, determine what types of wood work best in the creation of certain objects.

"When I find a piece of wood that strikes my fancy, I set it aside and let it age, while I let the idea about how I am going to use it simmer in my mind," Tom said. "I have awakened in the middle of the night and said, 'I know what I am going to do with that piece!' "

Of particular interest is wood containing a lot of burls or growths that result from injuries to the tree or shrub. Burls make excellent bases for choices for flower vases and decorative vessels.

"I try to preserve the natural character of the wood," Tom said. "I want to get the most beautiful effect from it that I can. The more distressed and worm eaten it is, the more I enjoy turning it."

But, Tom noted, the more distressed the wood, the harder it is to turn.

Working with various sizes and types of scrappers, Tom turns the wood to thicknesses that approach 1/8th of an inch. Because of the danger of trying to do too much at one time with a fragile piece of stock, Tom often works on a piece for a while and then sets it aside to work on something else.

"I have learned that patience is very important," Tom said. "I don't push it with the more fragile wood I enjoy using."

Once the piece has been turned to Tom's satisfaction, something he determines by sight and touch—rather than by measuring with a set of calipers—there remains the application of six coats of clear lacquer, a series of rubdowns with fine steel wool, and finally a coating or two of paste wax (hand buffed with soft cloths). This gives his pieces a smoothness that mimics the transparency of silk and the suppleness of a fine cashmere sweater.

The pieces range from spiral sculptures made from sassafras, to cherry burl winged vessels and maple vases that seem almost too fragile to touch. There are elements of the

Tom Frey turning a piece in his workshop

Photograph by Jerry Rhodes

Oriental and the American southwest in his designs, but he prefers to take each piece as it comes, working with nature to bring out the hidden beauty of the wood.

While Tom can work with pieces of wood approaching two feet in diameter, he also turns doll-house-sized sculptures that are popular with collectors who attend miniature shows. The materials used for these pieces range from the everyday to the exotic, including deer and moose antlers, dyed plywood and soapstone, as well as nuts with such exotic names as becarrio, brown rapphia, ivory balm, uxi kernal and zacchaeus.

Arts and fine craft shows afford a place for Tom to sell his creations and to see what his contemporaries are up to. "When Pat and I go to a show, we talk with other turners and we see if anybody has any new woods they are working with," Tom said. "Every wood turner, even the top name people, will tell you how they do things. I'm always interested in what others are doing, but I don't want to copy their work. I think it is best to do your own thing."

Tom has exhibited his work in both juried and invitational shows the length of the East Coast and as far west as Chicago.

Perhaps one of the most difficult things for Tom continues to be figuring out how much to charge for his creations.

His pieces range from $17 for a miniature vase to $1,800 for "Nature's Lace #XXII"—the latter is the 22nd vessel turned from a huge maple that was felled because of carpenter ant damage. He said pieces in the $45 to $125 range are his best sellers.

Tom and Pat meet a lot of people at various shows. Those who stand out are individuals looking for that perfect gift to give to that special someone.

"One person said he was looking for something nice to give to a couple as a wedding present," Tom said. "Later, he said the couple who received it said it was the best gift they got."

At another show, a woman shopping with her daughter kept looking at one of Tom's pieces, but was hesitant to make the purchase. When Tom asked her if she was interested, she told him she was indeed, but felt that she could not afford the particular item at that time. To her surprise, Tom told her that she could lay the piece away, just like a department store.

"She couldn't believe that it was possible to do this," Tom said. "The next year she came back and said she wanted a table made on which to display the piece she had brought the previous year."

For Tom, the most rewarding aspect of the whole creative adventure is that he continues to discover new ways to express the fascination with woodturning that began in junior high.

"Anyone can do this," Tom said. "The thing is to do it differently. I like the challenge. I like what I'm doing."

—*Jerry Rhodes*

Author's note: To contact Tom Frey, call him at (302) 732-6172 or send an e-mail to [pwftef@netzero.net], or send a note to Tom Frey, Woodturner, RD4 Box 45A, Marina Road, Dagsboro, DE 19939.

Clyde Roberts

Port Penn, Delaware

Working Waterman

Port Penn, Delaware, is a sleepy little fishing village, and most folks there seem to like it that way. Sitting at Clyde Roberts' kitchen table seemed appropriate, since the fisherman and long-time resident can serve up a smorgasbord of information on just about any topic associated with the quiet, historic water town.

Nestled along the banks of the Delaware River, the village has been home for generations of muskrat trappers, pile drivers, snapper catchers and crabbers plus farmers who work the neighboring countryside. But each passing season brings to the area more development, with bigger houses and wider highways and more traffic—all of which will eventually have a permanent effect on the residents and their all-too-quickly passing way of life.

Now 76, Clyde lives in what he calls the Commandant's House. The structure used to stand on nearby Reedy Island as part of a federal government quarantine station that was an immigration stop during the early years of the 20th century. Foreigners heading for the New World would have to stay at the facility until they were deemed healthy enough to be admitted into the United States or sent back home.

Clyde remembered growing up and visiting the island. "When I was 10 or 12 years old," he said, "I would go out there and spend the night on the island, with the caretaker. It was exciting to go over in the boat and sleep in that big house. I'll never forget it."

Eventually, some might say, that big house came across the river looking for Clyde. The federal government closed the quarantine facility and, in the 1950s, auctioned off the buildings. A local pile driver, Shelly Collins, bought it and a number of houses.

Ruth Ann, Clyde's wife, placed a half-century-old newspaper clipping on the kitchen table. They had come across the item and saved it in a scrapbook. The faded picture showed the house in which we were having our conversation. The headline read: "Eight-Room House Goes for a Boatride." The short story stated: "Without making a noticeable crack in the plaster, the eight-room, two-and-a-half-story home of the manager in residence of the former U. S. Quarantine Station on Reedy Island was moved yesterday by barge from the island to the mainland in Port Penn, in one piece."

"I tell you," Clyde said, "when the government builds something, it's top of the line. We've got slate and copper roofs and double plaster walls."

Speaking of the house, Clyde admitted that he is in charge of the outside decor. A large blue sideboard—with the word "Neptune" in gold lettering, from what is believed to be a Civil War-era ship—is attached to the front of his home. Assorted pieces of driftwood and thick boat lines serve as a sort of decorative nautical fence. Folk art replicas of a blue heron, a few pelicans and various ducks accent the property's entrance, boundaries and walkways.

"It has a bit of a nautical flair about it," Clyde said, pointing to his decorations. "I've been involved in fishing my whole life."

As he looked off into the distance, Clyde said, "When I was a little kid, I used to fish off of that bridge, and I used to have a notebook with a pencil. I would write everything that I caught—two eels, two perch, two catfish. I wish I had that book now. At the time I guess it was insignificant. But I was raised with fishing and snapping and trapping. I used to tend traps before I went to school."

And while visitors to the fishing town think they've discovered a quaint, quiet hideaway, the Port Penn area is nothing like it was when Clyde was a youngster.

"When I was a boy and came down here from Wilmington," he said, "there was only one restaurant open at night, on Route 13. Today, there are all these food places all over—McDonald's, Arby's.

"We're trying to preserve this town. This is a village. It's very unique, very small, and we like it that way. When you see developments surrounding you, it's unbelievable. Having been raised in this town, when you go out along the road and see what's been built, it's unbelievable to see the development the way it is now.

"Who knew at the time that lots that sold for $6,000 each would now be going for $50,000 each? If you knew and had the foresight, and had a lot of money, you could be rich now. But it's still quiet here in town."

A passing reference to his career with the U. S. Postal Service, from which he retired in 1981, opened up another well full of memories. Clyde recalled his years working out of the Philadelphia office of the RPO (Rail Post Office). In the 1950s, he would travel the rails along the length of Delmarva, from Philly to Cape Charles, Virginia, delivering and picking up and sorting bags of mail along the route.

"We would haul everything," Clyde said. "There were railcars filled with money. That was before the days of the Brinks armored cars. It was steam back in those days. And you would ride and the soot would get in your face."

Working three, 24-hour days on and seven days off gave Clyde opportunities to get in a fair amount of fishing. But when he thought of the layovers in small towns like Delmar, Pocomoke City and Harrington, the memories of his experiences caused him to laugh.

"There was this widow in Harrington," he said, shaking his head. "She charged one dollar a night, and the room was below zero. It was freezing and it was snowing outside. That room belonged in the stone ages."

By the time he was 55, Clyde retired from the post office to enjoy his second career, commercial fishing, but to him spending time on the water is more like recreation.

"I don't consider fishing a job," he said. "I love it. When fishing gets in your blood, it's a disease."

In the two hours that followed, Clyde talked of the old days when "herring was thick out there," just off the shore at nearby Augustine Beach. In those days, he said, there were no motors on boats and you could "fish in washtubs and catch them full of herring." He described small huts that were perched above the water's surface where fishermen lived year round. Then he talked about the sturgeon, how to find them and

Clyde in front of the Commandant's House, with his blue heron carving standing near the sideboard from the ship Neptune

how to net catch the prehistoric looking fish that can grow to over 18 feet and weigh 1,000 pounds.

Admitting that he gets out on the water as often as he can, Clyde said he and his wife, Ruth Ann, work well together, dropping 600-foot-long lengths of net and later performing a well-coordinated process of reeling them in and separating hundreds of fish from the mesh as quickly as possible.

Words like flood tide, slack tide and ebb tide, or sink net and haul seine, were sprinkled throughout his conversation. To a landlubber it was like trying to decipher a foreign language. But a commercial fisherman would know that the words referred to shifts in water current or the size and type of net. Each could mean the difference between the size of his catch or having no catch at all.

Then there's always the weather.

Mention the wind and the waves and Clyde talks of the fickleness of nature and the need for vigilance on even sunny days when the sea seems as calm as a sleeping babe.

"You have to respect the water," he said. "I respect it. I don't take anything for granted. A storm can come up at any time, without any warning. When the barometer drops and the sea is so calm you can hear a pin drop, it's time to head for shore."

When asked what advice he would give a novice fisherman, his response was quick and short.

"Don't go out alone," Clyde said, seriously. "It's a dangerous job and you should never go out alone."

Has he ever fished solo?

"Yes," he admitted, then added, "once I fell overboard and got tangled. I held onto the side of the boat and eventually worked my way out. I'm here, and I was lucky. I've gone out myself in the '70s. That was crazy. You have to respect the water. It can be friendly and it can be ferocious."

With decades of experience fishing on the Delaware, it's not surprising that he serves on a number of state and regional fishing advisory panels and committees, including the Atlantic States Marine Fisheries Association. At meetings and during informal conversations, he shares his knowledge and opinions about marine matters with biologists, naturalists, environmentalists and politicians.

"When you get involved in fishing," Clyde said, "if you can make some contributions to the advisory panels and help with the management planning, it's good to give your input. Management is the only way to go. You have to have that in order to maintain the stock and allow the fish to reproduce."

He acknowledged that there have been significant improvements in the water quality of the Delaware.

"When I was a boy," he said, "you could see oil and sewage so bad you could see sewage floating downriver. As far as looking at the water, it is cleaner now."

But, in the end, despite government management programs, pollution regulations and the best intentions of well meaning citizens and reports by overlapping committees and research studies, fishing and crabbing will never return to their long gone glory days. Progress, development and a swelling populace have taken their toll.

"Fishing is a dying industry," Clyde said. "In order to keep up with the growth of the world's population, aquaculture is coming on big time. That's the way it will be. There's more demand than there is supply. Fishermen just can't supply the world's demands."

Somehow, no matter what changes come to Port Penn or the fishing industry, one gets an indication that Clyde will continue heading out during the early mornings from the Commandant's House. And a short time later he'll be steering his boat, the *Ruth Ann,* along the Delaware—in search of sturgeon or perch or shad or rock, or whatever else is running— for as long as he is able.

"It's good therapy," he said. "When you're out at daybreak, and there's no one else there at all, it seems like the water is all yours. It's a great feeling."

Ray Russo

Earleville, Maryland

'The Last Mission'

This weekend, they'll have the Indianapolis 500. They'll start with 33 cars, go 500 miles and be lucky if 10 can finish the race. They have the best mechanics in the world. Here we were, a civilian army that worked on airplane engines. We had 143 planes that went 3,800 miles apiece without having a problem and all of them made it back."

That's how Ray Russo, 84, now a resident of Crystal Beach Manor, Maryland, compared the annual Memorial Day weekend auto race to the final air bombing mission of World War II.

Ray was an aircraft and engine specialist with the rank of sergeant in the Army Air Corps stationed in Guam when the war ended. Now, after nearly 60 years since that August day his plane—*Punchin Jody*—left the landing strip, he said he's satisfied that the story of The Last Mission is being told.

In mid May and during Memorial Day weekend, The History Channel televised a two-hour program about the little known bombing mission over Japan that took place on Aug. 14-15, 1945. Ray taped the program and said it was very accurate, probably because it was based on the book *The Last Mission*, co-written by Jimmy Smith, one of the airmen in Ray's squadron.

A barber from Bryn Mawr, Pennsylvania, Ray and his wife, Dee, bought a summer cottage in Cecil

County in 1980. Fifteen years later, they became permanent residents.

The conversation of war experiences long passed, but not forgotten, took place in Ray's Memorabilia Room. The two-car garage-size structure behind his house is filled with photographs of flight crews and certificates reinforcing his military memories. A large American flag dominates the room near a table covered with books on World War II. As expected, one is entitled *The Last Mission*.

"A copy of this book should be in every school," Ray said, holding the thick volume in his hand.

With the expertise of a man who had been there and done that, the barber turned mechanic for Uncle Sam pointed to the very large color photograph of the airplane about which he received more than three years of intensive training—the four-engine, B-29 Super Fortress.

"We were ordinary Joes. I was a barber and I got excellent training," Ray said.

After every mission, Ray explained, his crew worked three to four days, more than 12 hours a day in 120-degree heat, completing maintenance on the plane, getting it ready for the next bombing run.

"When you see an airplane flying," he said, "you seldom think about the mechanics or about the ammo crew that loaded the bombs."

> *"You hear a lot about the first serviceman killed in the war, a lot about the raising of the flag on Iwo Jima. You hear about the atomic bombs that were dropped. Except you never hear about The Last Mission."*
>
> *—Ray Russo*

The B-29, he said, is 99-feet long with a 141-foot wingspan. It could carry 28 bombs weighing 500 pounds each or 164 incendiary bombs weighing 100 pounds each. As if he were back on the South Pacific tarmac beside his plane *Punchin Jody*, Ray continued to talk about the capabilities and dimensions of the aircraft that he still knows like the back of his hand.

"Up to the last mission, our longest, most of the flights were about 3,000 miles, over water. There's no gas station that you could stop in if you had a problem. We carried 8,600 gallons of fuel. That would just about get them there and back, if the flight engineer calculated it properly."

A member of the 315th Bomb Wing, with about 12,000 servicemen, Ray was in the 501st Bomb Group and the 485th Bomb Squadron. The 1,000 men in his squadron arrived in Guam in February 1945 and completed 15 missions. All of them were aimed at destroying Japan's fuel and energy facilities. A history of his unit contains a page detailing each mission, and the names of the targets tell the story: Utsobe River Oil Refinery, Kowasaki Petroleum Center, Nippon Oil Co. & Refinery, Ube Coal Liquefaction and Shimutsu Oil Refinery

The squadron's final bombing order was aimed at the Nippon Oil Refinery in Akita, located in the northwest corner of Japan. Ray said it was a 3,800 mile round trip. To add to each plane's fuel capabilities, the four turret guns were removed, leaving only

Just before heading overseas, Ray Russo (standing behind the barber chair), was ordered to give a haircut to each member of his squadron. Ray, a barber by trade, said he gave 300 cuts in two days and his clippers were so hot he had to wrap a wet towel around them to hold them in his hands.

Photograph provided by Ray Russo, from his collection

two .50 caliber machineguns to defend against Japanese attack aircraft—and only prayers and luck to avoid damage from heavy anti-aircraft fire.

The planes took off at 4 p.m., Aug. 14, got to their target at 1 a.m., and returned to the base on Guam at 8 a.m., Aug. 15. Every one of the 143 aircraft survived the 16-hour mission, Ray said. "Some of the planes were coughing when they were coming in to the runway, because they had run out of gas. A few had to be towed off the runway. That's how close they were to being out of fuel."

In the televised documentary, viewers also learn about how the blackout of Tokyo, caused by the over flight of the B-29s, helped thwart a coup attempt by Japanese officers that would have delayed that country's surrender and cost millions of Japanese and Allied lives.

Although the crews on the returning planes learned of the official surrender as they were flying back to Guam, Ray said the much anticipated news wasn't formally announced to the airmen until 10 a.m. that morning.

Ray paused a moment and lowered his head, turning it to the side. He was affected by the emotion associated with the vivid memories that he said he could see and feel after all the passing years. "We

laughed and cried and hugged, we were so excited. And our crew had come home."

When Ray returned from the war and worked in his barbershop, conversations about overseas experiences among customers, both civilian and former military, were commonplace. However, pride in his unit's major contribution soon turned to frustration when Ray discovered that he had to convince listeners that The Last Mission actually took place.

"They all would say, 'They dropped the first A bomb on Aug. 6 and the second A bomb on Aug. 9, and that was the end of the war!' And I would tell them we took off on the 14th of August and every one of ours got back the next day, and they'd say, 'What do you mean?' "

According to The History Channel documentary and the press release from Broadway Books, publisher of *The Last Mission,* up until very recently most Americans attributed Japan's surrender directly to the effects of the atomic bombs on Hiroshima and Nagasaki. But few people realized that between Aug. 9 and the surrender on Aug. 15, Allied forces engaged in nearly 1,000 individual B-29 combat missions across the home islands of Japan.

I asked Ray how many people knew about The Last Mission before the recent book and publicity.

"I never met anyone who knew about The Last Mission," he said. "Everybody is surprised."

After reading the book by his old flight squadron buddy Jim Smith, radio operator on the plane named *Boomerang,* and watching the documentary, Ray admitted he was satisfied that this significant story has been told.

"I was excited," the veteran said. "It was very accurate. I even saw some of my old buddies on there." Then Ray thought for a moment and added, "You hear a lot about the first serviceman killed in the war, a lot about the raising of the flag on Iwo Jima. You hear about the atomic bombs that were dropped. Except you never hear about The Last Mission."

Author's note: A similar version of this story first appeared in *The Cecil Whig.*

Members of the Punchin Jody *crew pose for a photograph on Guam in 1945. Ray Russo is standing at the far right.*

Photograph provided by Ray Russo, from his collection

Rick Fisher

Lancaster, Pennsylvania

'You're the Ghost Guy!'

They call him the "Ghost Guy." It doesn't seem to bother him. In fact, he said he's gotten used to it and sort of likes the label. At least it gets people's attention. But that's not difficult to do when they find out he's founder and president of the Pennsylvania Ghost Hunter's Society.

I met Rick Fisher at the Gettysburg Ghost Conference in 1998. He was there to talk about ghost photography, specifically how he captures paranormal images on film.

His material was fascinating, discussing the difference between an orb and an apparition, and providing details on how to distinguish between the similar manifestations of ectoplasm and car exhaust.

He offered tips on how to find haunted sites, and then he told the audience how to investigate the site properly. In particular, he stressed the need to keep detailed records and he offered information about the equipment needed if you wanted to head out and capture ghostly evidence on film.

During a conversation a few years later in Lancaster, Pennsylvania, Rick shared additional details about his life after dark—the best time to be out stalking for spirits.

Rick's entry into the spirited world of ghost hunting started in the early 1960s, when he was 7 years old. One night, he recalled seeing a figure of a man in a hallway of his grandmother's home.

"I was afraid to go to the bathroom," Rick said, "because of the dark figure I saw. Eventually, I found out that it probably was the spirit of my great grandfather."

That first paranormal experience stayed with Rick for the rest of his life. He also said that while growing up, he spent a fair amount of time reading a lot of ghost stories. Eventually, he followed his interests and, in 1997, he conducted an Internet search and discovered the International Ghost Hunter's Society web site. He joined the young organization, which at that time only had about 20 members. After attending his first ghost conference in Illinois in 1997, he learned the basics on how to take pictures and record evidence of spirit activity and energy. Those in the ghost research field call these objects "orbs," but to the untrained eye they look like small water spots in the background of photographs.

As time progressed, he began experimenting with new equipment that some believed would indicate a spirited presence. These included such electronics store, over-the-counter items as thermal scanners, electromagnetic field detectors and different types of cameras and flash accessories.

"I went to a cemetery by myself," Rick said, "a real old one. I didn't know what to expect. I was curious and a little scared. We all fear being alone in a cemetery, with the shadows and darkness. My awareness was high, and it was kind of eerie. But I just took pictures, went back, got them developed and looked at the results."

Rick said he found nothing unusual on the developed film, but he continued to search for evidence of spirits, mainly interested in capturing his first, very own "orb."

Opening a thick photo album, Rick flipped to a set of pages holding a number of pictures and pointed to a series of small, light colored dots that seemed to be floating above a row of old gravestones. He explained that ghost hunters believe that these light colored spheres indicate spirit—or ghostly—energy.

Investigators hope that someday they will be able to understand how to communicate with, or understand the origin and significance of orbs.

Rick said he began to seek out places that had well-known haunted reputations, figuring those sites would be ideal for discovering active spirits. Soon, people began talking about the "ghost guy" who spent his free time stalking cemeteries. This led to a newspaper article, which of course included a mention of the Pennsylvania Ghost Hunter's Society (renamed the Paranormal Society of Pennsylvania in 2003), which generated phone calls, more leads and interested people, which led to additional contacts, calls, interest and activity.

Thinking back, he said the newspaper stories continued, and they were followed by TV interviews, documentaries, radio talk shows, speaking presentations and now tours and workshops.

"They put my e-mail address and phone number in the article, and I got 30 calls and 40 e-mails almost immediately," Rick said. "When people asked about the society, I explained what it was and that it costs nothing to join. I still get so much e-mail it's hard to keep up with it."

Soon, Rick was inviting people he didn't even know to come into his home and attend meetings. Currently, he has about 500 members statewide operating in eight regional chapters. But he's most familiar with the 30 active members who live in the Lancaster region.

It didn't take long, he added, for his group to outgrow his home and cause him to move his monthly meetings to the Railroad House, a haunted restaurant and inn located in nearby Marietta, Pennsylvania, a small town near the Susquehanna River.

One evening each month, the Lancaster area participants get together and share photographs and experiences about investigating haunted houses and sites. The conversations are informative, anecdotal and instructional. But it's during several workshops that Rick also holds each year that he gives detailed information on the "how to" techniques needed to capture paranormal evidence on film.

He shares information on the equipment—plus its costs and sources—and shows the audience members how each item is used.

"What we teach," he said, "anybody can do and learn. I tell the techniques of ghost hunting so you can go out and do it."

At paranormal conferences, like the one he hosts in Gettysburg, Pennsylvania, Rick serves as a featured speaker and instructor. He stays awake for nearly three days straight, walking the battlefield, inspecting historic buildings and exchanging tales and techniques with other ghost hunters from around the country.

Rick (right), with author and publisher Troy Taylor, at the second annual Independent Ghost Conference held in Camp Hill, Pennsylvania, in 2003.

"When everyone's sleeping, I'm filming," he said. "When I go to a conference, I don't sleep."

Some of the material Rick has captured on film—and his comments during in-person interviews—have been featured on such programs as The Travel Channel's show *Secrets: Ghostly Gettysburg* and also on *The Pennsylvania Ghost Project.*

He has been featured in Mark Nesbitt's *Ghosts of Gettysburg* and has worked with a number of authors, including Dorothy Fiedel and Katherine Ramsland.

Ask him to share his most interesting experiences and he takes a few moments to decide where to begin. Could it be the voice he captured on tape that he heard calling him in a deserted cemetery one early morning, or maybe it was the video he took of three orbs moving across a room, but then there are the orb clusters in the centuries-old graveyard, or the circumstances surrounding those special photographs of apparitions and ectoplasm.

Of course, one of the best incidents is when he was working a graveyard late one evening and was stopped by a passing police car. Concerned that he might get involved in a hassle, Rick was careful to tell the officer very precisely that he was searching for spirit energy. To Rick's surprise and satisfaction, the officer became excited and said his wife loved the paranormal and was going to be thrilled when he told her about meeting Rick. They had read about his work in the local paper.

With more than 600 investigations behind him, Rick's worked in cellars and attics, opera houses and railroad tunnels, restaurants and battlefields, deserted mills and college dormitories—and everywhere there are the ghosts.

"Ghosts are everywhere," Rick said, smiling. "That's Dave Oester's phrase," he added, referring to the International Ghost Hunters Society founder. "There's also been activity reported at modern sites.

> *'When everyone's sleeping, I'm filming. When I go to a conference, I don't sleep.'*
> —Rick Fisher

That's when we have to ask what was on the land before? Could it be an Indian burial ground, a forgotten cemetery? And spirits aren't stationary," he added. "They're free to travel. They don't have to stay in one place."

Rick has gotten calls from enthusiastic ghosters and open-minded people with a serious interest in the paranormal. As expected, he's also received his share of criticism from those who condemn him and say he's doing the work of the devil.

"I also get strange e-mail from kids," he added, "and messages from people who want to test me, to see what I'll say. Someone once told me they took a shower and, instead of water, nothing but blood came out of the faucets. They wanted to know what they should do. 'Move!' I said. You have to be professional. If there is something that serious, there's nothing I could do about it.

"Most people just want to share their experiences with you. They say they want to be able to let someone know they live in a haunted house, and they'll give me their story and their name and I'll never hear from them again. It's a kind of therapy for them in a way."

One of the developments of which Rick is most proud is being the first ghost hunter to use a digital camera. Prior to this technological development, he said, investigators would have to take a picture, leave the scene and get the film developed. As a result, days would pass before hunters would know if they had captured any activity on film, or even if there was anything worthwhile at the site.

Now, with digital equipment, ghost photographers are able to see possible activity immediately. If there is, they can continue the investigation and save the image. If not, they can erase the digital image and reshoot. There's no need send out film for processing, and that saves both time and money.

Rick, who's known in the business as the "Father of Digital Ghost Photography," admitted that a serious ghost hunter could spend a fair amount of money on a growing range of sophisticated equipment.

But everyone has to have a hobby, and what hobby doesn't cost something?

However, he pointed out, the information that he provides has been used successfully by people who have taken photographs with a bottom-of-the-line, disposable camera. If there's sprit energy at a site, even a cheaper camera will be able to record it.

Since no one has yet captured a ghost in a jar, the question remains: Are there any substantive results from all these investigations?

"I think we're onto something," Rick said. "Before, we used to rely on psychics and spiritualists for leads and evidence. Now, with this new equipment, the photographs are giving us indications of spirit energy. We've come a long way in a short amount of time. Now we're beginning to get into EVP, electronic voice phenomena, capturing voices on tape. In five years from now, in 10 years from now, who knows what the possibilities will be? They'll come out with new equipment and someone will apply it to ghost hunting, and we're going to

have evidence and proof. I think we're close to unlocking the door to the spirit world."

The one occurrence that seems to bother Rick is when people call him a "ghostbuster."

"A lot of people think I can come in and bless a house," he said. "Nothing is farther from the truth. Ghostbusters are believed to remove spirits from a site, and we don't do that. We study spirits. We're trying to find evidence of paranormal activity."

Rick teaches courses on Paranormal Investigation at the Harrisburg Area Community College, he is publisher and editor of *Paranormal Pennsylvania & Beyond* magazine and he conducts the Ghosts of Marietta walking tour and Ghosts of the River Towns driving tour.

It isn't a surprise that he's developed both a nickname and a following. But does he like when people call him the Ghost Guy?

Rick smiled, then replied, "I guess. Everybody has to have a nickname."

Author's note: To contact Rick Fisher, send him an e-mail at [rfisher@redrose.net], visit his web site at [www.paranormalpa.com] or call him at (717) 871-8610.

The Last Picture Show

As you drive east through Dagsboro, Delaware, on your way to the Atlantic beaches, it's easy to overlook the Clayton Theatre—probably because it's not supposed to be there.

Everyone knows we're in the 21st century, and our movie houses are modern now. Today we go to multi-screen movie complexes that could easily have been designed by someone operating a cookie cutter—heavy on plastic and light on style, character and class. A national chain owns them, and its faceless management board makes all the decisions.

When you go to the cinemall, you probably will find something you'd like to see, after all, a different movie begins every 15 minutes. Oh, and they use the very latest state-of-the-art, high-tech, digital equipment, including advanced enhanced sound systems and recliners with cup holders for seating. That's the way it is today—impersonal and fast and convenient.

The old, more leisurely days of movie going—at the single screen, neighborhood theatre—are long gone and nearly forgotten. The familiar face behind the ticket window—along with the glowing, neon marquee proclaiming its distinctive name—have been tossed in the dustbin of small town America's history.

Photograph provided by Joanne and Ed Howe

Except on Main Street in Dagsboro.

Since 1949, the two-story, gray-and-pink, stone-front building has been the entertainment center of the community's life and, amazingly, it's still in operation, all year round.

In the beginning of 2001, Joanne and Ed Howe bought the historic movie house. After more than two years operating in the small community, they said they are proud to host the theatre's second half-century of operation.

The couple moved to Dagsboro in 1997. Ed, a local developer was working on the Village of Bethany Forest. Joanne was interested in owning her own business. They were attracted to the hometown atmosphere of Clayton and quickly became frequent patrons of the theatre.

Joanne, who is the primary operator of the theatre and adjacent video store, said there were signs that the Clayton was going to be an important part of her life.

"My father's name was Clayton," Joanne said. "He passed away in 1991 and the first time I saw the marquee with his name on it, it definitely caught my eye." As did the movie poster of John Wayne starring in *The Sands of Iwo Jima*, which was prominently displayed in the theatre lobby.

Joanne and Ed Howe

Dagsboro, Delaware

"My father was in the Navy during World War II," she said, " and became a medic's assistant for the Marines on Iwo. He never talked much about it, but I know the experiences he had on Iwo Jima stayed with him his entire life. Seeing the poster in the lobby and his name on the marquee was really just the beginning of a series of coincidences which seem to connect me to the theatre."

Ed recalled his initial impressions of the Clayton. "We had always liked going to the movies and fell in love with this old theatre the first time we came here. We would often comment on what a nice family owned business it was, but it never crossed our minds that they would ever sell it."

Joanne, who has a degree in communication arts from Salisbury State University, said she was searching the Internet in December 2000 for business opportunities and was shocked when she discovered the Clayton Theatre was for sale.

"It was two in the morning when I found it," she said, "and I was so excited I woke my husband to tell him."

The next day, the couple called the owners for an appointment to tour the property, and soon thereafter made an agreement to buy the historic complex, which included the Silver Screen video store adjoining the theatre.

Joanne worked with the previous owners, the Wilkins family (Ron Jr. and Sr.) to learn everything she could in a crash course on the movie house and video business.

"I knew absolutely nothing about the movie business," she said, smiling. "The Wilkins family worked with me for three weeks and helped me learn the basics I needed to know to run the business."

> *'There used to be single screen movie houses in many small towns around here. They have all been converted to churches or office buildings or torn down completely, but they have all disappeared. I think people are thrilled we're still here, and we're happy about it, too.'*
>
> *—Joanne Howe*

She learned everything from ordering inventory for the video store to making popcorn, from selling tickets to dealing with film distributors.

"It was definitely a whirlwind," she said, "and believe me, I'm still learning new things to this day, but that's what keeps it fun and interesting."

Over their two-and-a-half years of operation, Joanne said she and Ed have realized the theatre's importance to the community.

Built in 1948, the theatre opened on Feb. 2, 1949. The daughters of the builders and original owners gave Joanne a copy of the opening day program, billing the Clayton as "Sussex County's Newest and Most Modern Theatre." The grand opening featured the musical *One Touch of Venus*, starring Ava Gardner and Robert Walker. Adults could enjoy cartoons, newsreels and a feature film for only 50 cents, and children were charged a quarter.

"I was so excited when the ladies gave me the opening day program," said Joanne, who said she had been trying to find out the name of the first film ever shown in the theatre. Also, with her birthday being February 2, the opening date took on even greater significance.

While the movie house's main clientele comes from the community and nearby towns, a number of people who pass the theatre on the way back and forth from the beach stop in as well. Word of mouth seems to have generated a loyal and growing following, Joanne said. Also, the distinction of being one of the very few remaining single screen movie houses in the area attracts both movie buffs and customers looking for a chance to relive their early movie going experiences. Older customers also love sharing the hometown experience with their children and grandchildren.

"One of the first things we did after we took over," Joanne said, "was relight the neon marquee. It had not been totally relit for 20 years, and it was exciting for everyone in town to see the neon glowing once again. Some people told me they had lived here all their lives and had never seen it lit at all. It was certainly an event and we loved being able to make it happen."

Ed said they also offer little extras that add to their patrons' visit to the Clayton.

Each night after the showing of the movie *Chocolat,* they set up a table in the lobby with fudge and brownies for patrons leaving the theatre. For the showing of *Pearl Harbor* they played Big Band and Swing music through loudspeakers so people waiting in line for tickets could get into the mood for the movie. Some patrons even danced up to the window for their tickets. Ed and projectionist, Charlie Thorns, wore military uniforms during the run of the film.

Joanna Howe in the projection room

"We put a little different spin on going to the movies," Ed said. "If there's an opportunity for us to put some fun into coming here, we do it."

Walking through the building, Joanne pointed out that 90 percent of the interior decorations are original, including the classic wall covering and art deco lighting.

"We still use the original projectors that were installed in 1948," Joanne said. "The lamp housing has been updated, but the projector heads are original. We've purchased additional old projectors to use as back ups for spare parts."

Ed and Joanne said they are fortunate that Charlie Thorns, the projectionist, has stayed on. He has been in the business since he was 8 years old and has been at the Clayton for almost 20 years. He knows run to operate and care for the projectors and has showed her how to do it.

The Clayton has 316 seats on its main floor. The balcony is closed but can accommodate an additional 140 seats. The original seats were replaced with some from the same period that were bought from an old Washington, D.C., movie house that was being torn down. The original balcony seats were removed by the previous owners, but Joanne said they get a lot of requests from patrons who would like to sit up there. Someday, Ed and Joanne hope to reopen the balcony for seating.

The concession stand, Joanne said, was added many years ago and was not originally part of the movie house. Patrons originally went to the Cut Rate pharmacy and soda fountain next door for candy and sodas before the shows. Today, a fully stocked snack bar offers, beverages, candy and, of course, freshly made popcorn.

"Ed is in charge of popcorn," Joanne said, smiling.

Agreeing, her husband said, "I'm an expert in that department and I occasionally sell tickets."

Certainly, not too many people own a movie house. When the topic comes up in conversation, the Clayton Theatre owners agree their situation is either a pause maker or icebreaker.

"Owning a movie theatre is a good conversation starter," Joanne acknowledged.

Ed nodded and smiled as he tried to explain the reactions he's received to the couple's connection with the small town movie house.

"When people introduce me," Ed said, "they don't say, 'He's a developer.' They say, 'Ed and his wife own the Clayton Theatre!' People don't expect that. They like the fact that there are people they know who own a theatre. Most theatres are owned by companies and chains with tens or hundreds of screens."

One gets the impression that running the Clayton is not really a job, but more like a dedication to preserving a slice of small town history and culture.

"We read stories all the time," Ed said, "about theatres that are being restored and revitalizing small towns by creating art and entertainment centers. We have read about many of them being funded by art groups or foundations with government grants or funding. But we're doing this on our own, and I take pride in what we have here."

Ed also said that the public is fascinated with Hollywood and the movies. The local theater is the average person's link with the stars.

"I challenge you to tell me anybody who doesn't like movies or movie theatres," Ed said. "They might not like a certain movie, but no one doesn't like a movie theatre."

"This is the center of attraction in the town. This theatre has touched everyone who has lived here in some way. They met their girlfriend here. They had their first kiss in the balcony here. They bring their kids here now. And everybody in town has a story about this place."

Joanne agreed and smiled. "People come to the theatre and tell us stories all the time, and we love hearing them. The good and the bad. The stories of romantic stolen kisses in the balcony, and the stories of those who were thrown out for tossing things from the balcony on those below."

Ed shared the tale about his plumber who was banned from the theatre as a child because he snuck a dead porcupine into the building.

"During the movie," Ed said, smiling, "the 'dead' animal woke up and the management had to empty the theater."

Not surprisingly, the prankster was banned from the premises.

"These stories are a part of the history of Dagsboro," Ed said.

"I think the people in town appreciate that we kept the place open," Joanne said. "There used to be single screen movie houses in many small towns around here. They have all been converted to churches or office buildings or torn down completely, but they have all disappeared. I think people are thrilled we're still here, and we're happy about it, too."

Author's note: For information or to contact the Clayton Theatre, call (302) 732-3744 or visit the web site at [www.TheClaytonTheatre.com].

> *The local theatre is the average person's link with the stars.*

Jack and Gemma Buckley

Wilmington, Delaware

A Real Bookstore

When was the last time you were in a bookstore? Before you answer, understand that I'm talking about a "real" bookstore, not one of those coast-to-coast, several thousand exactly alike, cookie-cutter ones that you find in modern malls. And it's certainly nothing like the huge, supermarket-size variety, with a fancy coffee bar and pastries, and couches and sections offering non-book products like CDs and videos and electronic games.

I mean a bona fide, old-fashioned bookshop, that sells, well . . . books.

It's a place where the owner actually works there, operating the store with a spouse and relatives and probably a few reliable employees (who have been there so long that they're considered family).

In the 21st century, it's a rare type of establishment where the workers recognize their customers and probably know a lot of them by name. The atmosphere is different, too. It's not hurried or rushed, and the buyers and sellers often share a few pleasant moments at the counter, conversing about books and authors and community news.

Have you been in one of these friendly family bookstores lately?

Probably not. They're hard to find.

But if you want to savor a sense of shopping that was commonplace in the past, pay a visit, and be sure to buy a few books, at the Ninth Street Book Shop in downtown Wilmington, Delaware.

It's run by Jack and Gemma Buckley, two ex-school teachers, now in their fifties, who were quite happy in their jobs. In fact, they said they never had

any burning desire to get into the book business, until one day when they happened to notice an item in the newspaper.

"It was around Christmas time," Gemma said. "I was looking in the newspaper and noticed that the Paperbook Gallery was for sale. And I said to Jack, 'Wouldn't it be neat to own a bookstore?' "

A month later, in January 1977, they had decided to buy the store. In a very short amount of time they arranged for their relatives to provide help when necessary, and they worked like crazy after school and on weekends to get their new enterprise ready. On February 14, Valentine's Day, the two teachers opened for business in a narrow Orange Street storefront

That was a quarter century ago. But in the winter of 2003, while recalling the ups and downs and expansions and moves and major changes in the book business, Gemma and Jack seemed to be able to see vividly the events and memories that they shared.

Over the years, the couple's book business has operated at four downtown Wilmington locations. They took over the center city Greenwood Book Shop in 1983. And, from that year until 1993, they actually operated two bookstores—the present Ninth Street outlet and the Scrivener, which was located in the Grand Opera House on nearby Market Street.

They've seen their initial 1977 inventory of about 3,000 assorted volumes at the first store grow to its present size of 100,000 plus.

Obviously enjoying the opportunity to recall the highlights of their business, Gemma said, "Our kids grew up in the store. We even had the kids with cribs in here while we worked."

But like so many other independent businesses in cities across the country, their bookstore business has felt the effects of changes in the downtown workforce and staff reductions by major employers.

Over the years, Jack said, he and Gemma have seen how closely their small business is affected by decisions made in corporate boardrooms and government offices only a few blocks away.

"Up until the mid 1980s, there was a wall of people in here each day, particularly at lunch time," Gemma said. "The decline started in 1988, when the *News Journal* [newspaper, located a half block away] left. And when DuPont made its first big cutback, we could see the effect in our store that very day it was announced in the paper."

Jack explained that the major reduction in shopping wasn't because people had lost their jobs. Instead it was the effect of a sense of apprehension and uncertainty that spread rapidly throughout that large downtown chemical giant's headquarters.

More recently, the transfer of hundreds of public employees to the newly built courthouse—now located at the other side of downtown—has relocated more customers farther away from the Buckleys' doorway.

Despite these apparent setbacks, the Buckleys maintain a positive attitude, probably because they still love what they do—dealing in books.

"This is a great product," Jack said. "There's such a diversity of products here. I can't think of any other business like it in terms of sheer variety. The only thing close to a bookstore is a hardware store. And there you've only got about four to five thousand items to choose from. Here we have so much to chose from."

Jack said there are new titles coming out every day, so many in fact that he can't keep track of them all.

That variety, and constant influx of new material, plus the people make the job fun, he said.

"We've become friends with many of our customers," Gemma said, "and that's one of the best parts of this."

"Hand selling," is one of Jack's joys. That's when he turns a reader onto a book that he has enjoyed and is eager to pass onto another.

"I enjoy," Jack said, "the satisfaction I get back from putting a book into a person's hands."

Gemma agreed, mentioning that she often will come back from the beach and promote a "hidden treasure" that she enjoyed reading.

> *'I enjoy the satisfaction I get back from putting a book into a person's hands.'*
> —Jack Buckley

The magic of a bookstore is that it's a place where new discoveries are shared. Each day, parcels of knowledge are carried out the Ninth Street Book Shop's door. Some contain the words of a long dead author, others feature award-winning photographs and many provide new recipes that will delight diners for generations to come. For every reader, there's a special book that has meaning and purpose.

Even their six-day-a-week workplace is dramatically different from traditional office cubicles and modern sterile desk units. The Buckleys' store is accented with a unique wallpaper background provided by book spines that form a mass of intermingling hues and designs. This multicolored scene glides along corridors of bookcases and shelves, all containing volumes of works on endless topics, from art, music, romance, poetry, entertainment, travel and gardening to mystery, history, home improvement, language, politics, technology and adventure.

A bookworm accidentally locked inside this reader's heaven for the weekend probably would be thrilled rather than frustrated.

Of course, the owners have their personal preferences. Jack said he likes a good thriller and books on photography. For Gemma, cookbooks and biographies are preferred.

Keeping track of inventory has changed immensely since they first checked their shelves in 1977. Gemma recalled how Jack carried a thick wad of papers, with each indicating the sales history of a particular book. Today, a much more efficient computer program makes that cumbersome but functional record system seem archaic.

Since most employees today work for large companies, Jack and Gemma said that when people find out they own and operate a bookstore, certain questions are sure to be asked.

"They ask how you survive," Jack said, smiling. "They also admit that they like the idea that we can write our own paycheck and that we never have to consult anybody for anything—except our customers."

After working with books, authors and publishers for a quarter century— and surviving the decline in the downtown retail climate—the Buckleys have maintained a good sense of humor. Of course, this upbeat attitude has been aided by the antics, demands and quirks of some of their customers.

Mary Pierce, who has worked with the Buckleys for 25 years, said, "After all these years, there's always a memorable experience that makes it a joy to come to work. It's never boring."

Jack smiled and agreed, "We have an open door to the world, and we do meet the public. We've seen two or three bank robberies, and we've seen fights break out in front of our window over a parking space."

Nodding, Gemma added, "We've been robbed. I've chased down shoplifters. Nothing strikes us as unusual."

Since the Buckleys' shop is located a block from Wilmington's Playhouse Theater, over the years, touring actors have stopped in to buy reading material.

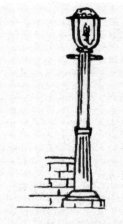

ninth street book shop

104 W. 9th Street
Wilmington, DE 19801
(302) 652-3315
Fax (302) 652-3371
E-mail: jackbuck@aol.com

Among their celebrity buyers are Vincent Price, Ann Davis, of *The Brady Bunch*, and comedian Tim Conway.

Ann Rule, who wrote a bestseller about the Capano murder trial, was a frequent visitor and held two book signings at the Ninth Street Book Shop after the release of *And Never Let Her Go.*

Gemma said that she and Jack helped the author proofread the book. And, while the book was heading to press, Gemma discovered an error, called Rule and they stopped the presses to make the correction.

But the secret of their personal and business success seems to be something beyond the merchandise they sell and the friends they have met.

This last-of-its-kind bookshop is unusual because it represents a time when people could turn the dream of a family business into a reality. For two and a half decades, the Buckleys have kept their venture alive.

That's no small achievement, especially in today's world where corporate giants make the rules and salivating government officials eagerly throw tax breaks at the feet of conglomerates that need financial help the least.

"We raised our family here," Gemma said. "And some of our employees have become like family. We value these relationships."

"But what we love most is working together," Jack said.

Agreeing, Gemma added, "If we ever closed this place, we would have to find a way to work together or to do something together."

Photograph by Greg Ositko

Bob Trapani Jr.

Lewes, Delaware

Keeping the Light Burning

B ob Trapani, of Lewes, Delaware, is passionate about lighthouses. Just mention these sturdy structures that stand in the waters beside the First State, and Bob can tell you something about each of the beguiling beacons. He also is well aware of the public's fascination, throughout the world, with these silent sentinels.

"Lighthouses mean many things to many people," Bob said. "Whether romanticizing about a bygone era, marveling at the strength of the lighthouse against the tempest, associating a spiritual connotation of a light against the darkness or symbolizing a person's love for the coast, lighthouses penetrate people's innermost emotions."

He also knows their history— their current status as operating or non-operating aids to navigation— and, most importantly, the kind of shape they are in.

It is this concern with the restoration and preservation of these life-saving towers that led Bob, a former Pennsylvania resident who visited the Delaware beaches, to establish the Delaware River & Bay Lighthouse Foundation (DRBLHF). The volunteer group is committed to advocating and carrying out restoration efforts that help preserve historic Delaware River and Bay lighthouses.

"I wanted to get more involved in the field of maritime preservation, so in 1999, I formed the Delaware River and Bay Lighthouse Foundation," Bob said. "We then pursued a lease of the Harbor of

> *'Lighthouses were built for just one purpose —to save lives. Now, it's the lighthouses that need saving.'*
>
> —*Bob Trapani Jr.*

Refuge Lighthouse, located about a half mile off of Cape Henlopen."

That same year, Bob also began serving on the board of directors of the Delaware Seashore Preservation Foundation (DSPF), which is responsible for the Life Saving Station near the Indian River Inlet. He was named executive director of the non-profit organization in July 2000.

He explained that his fascination with lighthouses began when he started coming to the Delaware resorts in the mid-1990s. The interest turned into a serious commitment shortly after the 38-year-old native of Pottstown, Pennsylvania, and his wife, Ann, relocated their family to Sussex County and became Lewes residents in 2000.

"I was interested in more than just the entertainment scene at the beach," Bob said. "I was interested in the history of the people and the place—it just snowballed from there."

It was only natural that Bob and his co-volunteers at the DRBLHF would be to turn their philanthropic preservation efforts towards the renewal and restoration of the historic Harbor of Refuge Lighthouse.

Sitting on a huge stone breakwater wall off Cape Henlopen, the lighthouse is the third incarnation of the original 30-foot, white frame tower that was built in 1902, and was powered by an optical "five-day" lens lantern that gave off a red light to warn mariners in the early years of the 20th century.

In 1908, a white, hexagonal, three-story building was erected, but a series of storms from 1918 through the early 1920s pretty much put the lighthouse out of commission.

At more than double the height of the original structure, the current 76-foot tower was originally powered by a four-panel, mechanically driven lens, which has been replaced with a solar-powered optic that gives off a pulsating white light that flashes every 10 seconds and can be seen for nearly 20 miles.

Harbor of Refuge Light Station was fully automated in 1973 and remained virtually uninhabited until the DRBLHF began restoring the structure during the summer of 2002.

"The Coast Guard could not step forward to help preserve lighthouses, due to budget constraints and more pressing concerns, and there wasn't any organized effort in Delaware to do anything about it," Bob said. "We received a recommendation from the Coast Guard in 2000, and in 2002 we officially signed a 20-year historic lease with them."

The glamour of the light had been long gone when Bob and his volunteer colleagues first entered the sealed up structure.

Bob Trapani at work on the upper portion of the lighthouse

Photograph by Lois Podedworny

"I remember it seemed like a place long forgotten by time," Bob said. "There was no light and the windows were boarded up—everything was dark, damp and musty smelling. The atmosphere inside the light was gloomy. You knew the lighthouse still served a purpose as an aid to navigation, but the human element had long been removed."

The hard work of the crew helped restore a sense of life to the light.

"One sight that is somewhat humorous," Bob recalled, "is seeing everyone at the end of any workday hobbling around and exhausted. Crew members have creaking knees, bad backs and tired muscles that they rarely use otherwise. So the sight of a dozen passionate individuals struggling to wrap up a hard day of work by coaxing their bodies to move along is humorous, but also extremely inspiring since everyone always gives everything they have."

When Bob and the crew first saw the light up close, he said they were awed at its size.

"You don't realize how massive the structure is from a boat or passing by it on the ferry," Bob said. "Upon closer examination, we began to gain an understanding of how harsh of an environment the lighthouse is situated in. People don't realize how horrendous the seas and winds can be out at the light.

"The scars of past battles with Mother Nature are quite evident. The light's steel superstructure is forever affected by the corrosive and destructive powers of the sea. Everywhere you look inside and outside the lighthouse, you can see visible, even alarming, signs of deterioration. The sight of the deterioration is quite humbling and daunting. Nonetheless, we use this horrible evidence as motivation to help save the lighthouse."

Bob said there are stories associated with every lighthouse, but since so many are automated it's becoming more rare to learn of events from those who actually worked at the lights. However, sometimes there are opportunities to hear experiences from those who lived them. Here is one such story.

"Stephen Jones was a former light keeper at Harbor of Refuge," Bob said, "and he happened to be stationed on the light during the great storm of March 1962. He revisited the light for the first time in 40 years, in March 2002. Stephen recounted how the storm lashed out at the lighthouse and made the keepers wonder if they were going to survive the ordeal.

"A rogue wave broke a second floor window in the lighthouse and deposited about an inch or two of water all over the hardwood floors. Another wave pushed water into the light and shorted-out the radio—eliminating the keeper's ability to communicate with the outside world. Later, the lights inside the light went out thrusting the keepers into a world of complete darkness and chaos. Canned goods were falling off the shelves. Furniture was vibrating across the floor, and the light seemed to shake after each massive wave slammed against the structure.

"Even the breakwater was completely under water. Mr. Jones recounted that for a few harrowing hours, they weren't sure they were ever going to make it off the light alive."

Having secured permission to carry out preservation efforts at the Harbor of Refuge Light Station, the first task was removing covers placed over the windows three decades earlier.

Volunteers at work on the Harbor of Refuge Light

Photograph by Lois Podedworny

"This was important, because it allowed light to come in, and moisture to go out," Bob said. "There was also the safety aspect. We had to make the dock and the lighthouse safe for both the visitors and volunteers."

Before the DRBLHF could even think about bringing visitors from the mainland out to tour the lighthouse, the landing dock at the Harbor of Refuge Light Station would have to be updated and secured.

"The Coast Guard installed a fiberglass landing dock, but with the bad ice storms of the winter of 2002-03, ice floes from upriver took the dock out," Bob said. "We replaced it with pressure-treated wood to make it as safe as possible."

After nearly a year of hard work, often in weather to match, the volunteer group successfully completed what Bob called "30 years worth of clean-up" and the first ever-public tour of a Delaware Bay lighthouse took place in June 2003.

While still working on the Harbor of Refuge project, the DRBLHF is in the process of applying for historic leases on the Liston Range Rear Lighthouse and the Reedy Island Rear Range Lighthouse, both land-based structures in New Castle County.

Bob said he views the restoration of lighthouses as being a combination of hands-on involvement, avocation and an educational enterprise for volunteers and visitors alike. And, he realizes it takes a community effort to make the thing work.

"Our whole mission is lighthouses, and to do this you have to create a team that is both talented and passionate about what they are doing," Bob said. "You also have to educate people about why it is important to save lighthouses. You have to make people see that what they are supporting has value. This is the biggest challenge faced by all preservation groups.

"We won't build anything like them again. It's vitally important that our youth understand and cultivate an appreciation for lighthouses. These sentinels stand in tribute to the sacrifice, achievement and prosperity of our great nation."

While Bob remains committed to lighthouse restoration and making the work part of a larger community consciousness, his volunteer efforts hardly stop here.

In 2000, Bob began working with the Aids to Navigation Team Cape May, and joined Flotilla 82 Cape May of the Coast Guard Auxiliary. Besides serving as an associate member of the Mariners Advisory Committee for the Bay and River Delaware, Bob works part-time at the Cape Henlopen Ship Reporting Tower as a vessel dispatcher for the Maritime Exchange for the Delaware River and Bay.

He also enjoys writing. In addition to serving for a year as editor of *Atlantic Light House Magazine*, he continues to share his maritime activities and lighthouse preservation efforts with the public in a variety of formats, including newspapers, magazines and the DRBLHF web site [www. delawarebaylights. org].

"I want to create a lasting impression," Bob said. "The bottom line is, I want to help save our heritage, not only in the physical sense, but for the future as well. We hope that our hard work will spawn a future generation of lighthouse restorers."

When asked why he and his co-volunteers at the DRBLHF chose what many would be symbols of an age that has come and gone, Bob offers this explanation: "Lighthouses were built for just one purpose—to save lives. Now, it's the lighthouses that need saving."

—*Jerry Rhodes*

Author's note: To contact Bob Trapani, call (302) 644-7046 or send an e-mail message to [info@delawarebaylights. org]. For information on the Delaware River and Bay Lighthouse Foundation, visit [www. dealwarebaylights. org]. For information on the Delaware Seashore Preservation Foundation (Indian River Life Saving Station), visit [www. indianriverstation. org].

Indian River Life Saving Station

Bob's full-time job is executive director of the Delaware Seashore Preservation Foundation (DSPF), headquartered in the restored Indian River Life-Saving Station Museum—located on Route 1, just north of the Indian River Inlet Bridge. The DSPF is a non-profit organization dedicated to the preservation and educational interpretation of the historic Indian River Life-Saving Station Museum.

The museum is open year round and a popular stop for many summer vacationers and tour groups. Built in 1876, the station was one of the first established along the treacherous Delaware coastline.

The United States Life-Saving Services, which saved 177,000 lives during its 44-year history, was merged with the Revenue Cutter Service in 1915 to form today's United States Coast Guard.

The Coast Guard used the Indian River Life-Saving Station until the Nor' easter of March 1962 caused the bay and the ocean to meet and left four feet of sand throughout the interior of the building while destroying outbuildings on the ground.

In 1996, a group of concerned citizens, led by founding chairman Clinton Bunting, started the movement that later became the Delaware Seashore Foundation.

Bob also is the author of *Indian River Life Saving Station . . . Journey Along the Sands, The U.S. Life-Saving Service Years, 1976-1915.* (See book cover below.)

For Bob, working at the Indian River Life-Saving Station complements his volunteer efforts with the Delaware River and Bay Lighthouse Preservation Foundation.

"I am a person who likes challenges," Bob said. "For me, it's a unique opportunity to make a difference in the local heritage. It's not really work; it's a labor of love."

—Jerry Rhodes

INDIAN RIVER LIFE-SAVING STATION . . .
JOURNEY ALONG THE SANDS
THE U.S. LIFE-SAVING SERVICE YEARS, 1876-1915

U.S. LIFE SAVING STATION Nº

BY ROBERT TRAPANI JR.

Photograph by Jaime Cherundolo

Victoria Lusardi (left) with her lifelong friend Audrey Brooks

Victoria Lusardi
Newark, Delaware

Delaware's First Beauty Queen

The two women sat on the built-in porch, talking of days past and pleasant memories. The younger one was petite, chubby and wore a blue cotton shorts-and-shirt suit, complete with sneakers and white socks. The other woman, taller and extremely lean, barely filled her chair. Her nylon covered ankles were crossed, her hands rested in the lap of her silk, pink-and-green floral pantsuit.

Although gray and aged, they smiled often, and each spontaneous grin revealed the wrinkles that years of happiness and sorrow had etched into their skin.

The afternoon's conversation followed an entertaining pattern of naming events, disagreeing over the details that surrounded them, then grabbing hands as they laughed once the particulars were finally resolved.

It is easy to confuse facts at their age, even easier to get frustrated with one another and with themselves when they can't recall things they want to remember. Yet, they do remember their more than 70 years of friendship, and nothing, not even a little disagreement over who's right, can cause them to forget their special bond.

The topic of the meeting was beauty, something these women felt they hardly portrayed at their advanced ages. Yet, from the interviewer's perspective, they both radiated loveliness with each syllable they breathed.

The taller lady, 87-year-old Ms. Victoria Lusardi, was Delaware's premier beauty icon. In 1933, at 5 feet, 7 inches and 126 pounds, an 18-year-old, born Victoria George, was crowned the first Miss Delaware.

"I got into it [the beauty pageant] by dancing," Victoria said. "We would always go dancing. Black Cat on Rt. 40 was where it all started. We didn't mess with anyone but the big boys, honey. Cab Calloway, Blanche Calloway and Paul Whiteman; swell bands."

Her lifelong friend, Mrs. Audrey Brooks, 80, helped Victoria recall the small details that a failing memory had stolen.

"Black Cat was a nice place," said Audrey. "It was a big building with a restaurant and a dance hall and people would usually go a few times a month."

"It used to be one of the best around here," Victoria agreed. "That Paul Whiteman was always tuned up. Wasn't he Audrey?"

"Yes, a bunch of people drank and got 'tuned-up' but not us," her friend replied, referring to nights she and Victoria spent dancing together at the Black Cat.

Audrey said she was only 11 when the following event occurred that changed Victoria's life.

Victoria recalled the scene. "One night when I was there they came into the crowd and asked who wanted to be Miss Delaware," she remembered. "All us girls got on stage and lined up. That was just the semifinals."

Victoria said talent had little to do with the competition and admitted the winner was chosen almost solely on appearance.

"I think it was a combination of your poise, your shape and your age," the older woman continued, pointing toward her college-age interviewer.

Victoria said she couldn't recall how many girls competed and that she was probably too wrapped up in the moment to even have noticed. " I was worried about Vicki," she said, referring to herself. "Never mind about them."

Although not able to be there the night her friend was crowned, Audrey remembered what made her lifelong friend stand out from the crowd.

"There weren't many girls as pretty as Vicki," Audrey said. "She had the most beautiful jet black hair. It was so curly. She always had beautiful hair. And she had a nice shape, too."

Victoria said that although like today, poise, shape and age had a lot to do with who was chosen to represent beauty when she was awarded Miss Delaware, some things have changed drastically since her time.

"We never tried to be sickly thin, like these girls today," she said.

"That's right," Audrey added, "when we went to school no one was on a diet. No one even knew what a diet was. There was only one fat girl in our class and that's because she had a thyroid problem. It's probably because we had to walk everywhere we went, huh Vic?"

"Yes we did," Victoria agreed. "Today I try to eat to gain some weight, I'm so thin, but it just doesn't work," she said, adjusting her freshly cut silver-blue hair, which offered hints of its majestic jet-black past.

The money spent trying to find a dress is another thing Victoria said has changed since she was crowned. "I didn't do much shopping from here to there like

Victoria in the 1930s

they do now. You had to wear what you had."

"Mostly, when we didn't make things, we shopped at Wilmington Dry Goods, a huge store that had everything," Audrey said. "It wasn't second-hand or anything. It was all new, but just not expensive."

"Yeah, and we were lucky if we got to Wilmington Dry, weren't we, Audrey?" Victoria replied.

Her modest, hard-working upbringing kept her busy, too busy for daydreams of being a beauty queen. "I would see other beauty queens come to town in parades and things and think, 'Wow, she looks nice,' but I never cared too much about it. I was too busy helping my father and working down at the mill."

Victoria Lusardi was born on Aug. 5, 1914, to Mr. and Mrs. Octavio George, and was one of five girls. They had one brother. The family lived in a small bungalow, which still stands on the corner of Wilbur Street and North Street in downtown Newark. Victoria, who was the second oldest, often had a lot to keep her busy.

"My father was a laborer during the day and had a large vegetable garden and bake shop on the side to make extra money," she said. "He would grow all the vegetables and make the baked goods, and I would drive a big truck to Wilmington for him and sell them.

"I worked down at the mill that used be on South

Chapel Street, too. So I didn't have much time to worry about looking pretty and being a beauty queen."

Audrey, who also grew up in Newark, said the close-knit community was what brought the two of them together.

"There were just a few families in Newark then and everyone knew each other," Audrey said. "I've known Vicki a long time, saw her win Miss Delaware, knew her when she had the sub shop and raised our kids together."

Besides being the first Miss Delaware, Victoria is also one of Newark's earliest entrepreneurs. In the mid 1930s, she and her sister Josephine started the popular former Angie's Sub Shop, now Wilbur Street Sub Shop. Victoria said it was one of the first places in town for delicious Italian food. "We sold subs for 39 cents and plates of spaghetti and meatballs for only a quarter."

Today, Victoria occupies a quaint apartment overtop the sub shop she once started and rents out the business to new store owners.

"The tenants are very nice," she said, "but the best thing is when I get hungry I just go right downstairs for the best wings and fries in town."

The walls of Victoria's apartment are covered with pictures taken of her with more recent Miss Delaware winners. Her car, which usually sits idle in the driveway, has a "1933 Miss Delaware" license plate on the front. Furniture drawers are filled with paper clippings of articles written about her.

"They all come and visit me, honey," she said, "Miss Delawares, reporters, you name it. I don't know what they want with an old woman like me."

Every year, Victoria is invited to attend the Miss Delaware pageant to take a picture with the new Miss Delaware.

"They always want to meet me because I was the first, but they usually can't even tell who I am until someone points it out," Victoria said, laughing at the notion that someone would recognize her today as a beauty queen.

Victoria sat for a while, not talking, staring into the distance, looking at the house where she had lived as a child and the sub shop she had started as a young woman. Her soft, pale and nearly flawless skin, despite her age, glistened as a single tear fell from her right eye. A radiant blue could be seen from behind a pair of clear plastic oval glass frames. It was hard to tell from the expression on her face whether she was happy or sad.

"It's terrible getting old, isn't it Audrey?"

"Sure is honey," her friend agreed. "But I'll tell you one thing, at least we're still here."

"Amen to that," Miss Delaware replied.

—*Jaime E. Cherundolo*

Writer's note: Victoria Lusardi passed away on March 17, 2003. She is survived by her sister Mary, her daughters, Connie and Jeannie, and her sons, Victor and George. Her presence will forever be missed, but she will live on in her family and friends' memories as one of the greatest women this region has ever seen. She truly was a queen of beauty. It is my hope that this piece will help us retain some of Vicki's character—the perfect mix of strength and humor we all need so much.

About the writer: Jaime E. Cherundolo of Newark, Delaware, is a 2003 graduate of the University of Delaware journalism program. Originally, this story was submitted as her final examination project in a feature writing course. Her story "Ghosts in the Cotton Field" appears in *Ghosts*, published by Myst and Lace Publishers Inc. in 2001.

Members of the Kelton Afternoon Ladies' Club (from left) are Jean Steele, Margaret Hickman, Polly Barnes, Anne McMahon, Beth Thomas and Betty Hannum.

Kelton Afternoon Ladies' Club

Kelton, Pennsylvania

Last of the Ladies

We met in the parlor of Betty Hannum's home, on a summer Saturday morning, in the village of Kelton, Pennsylvania. The small hamlet sits off a secondary road that intersects with U. S. Route 1. Unless you're looking for the town, you wouldn't know it exists. There's a small post office, and a number of old-style suburban houses sitting along quiet lanes. A first-time visitor almost expects to see Wally and the Beaver or Ozzie and Harriet's boys running around the well kept hedges on the corner. Six members of the Kelton Afternoon Ladies' Club were seated in a semicircle. They seemed happy to have an excuse to gather together before the group's next scheduled meeting.

In the adjoining dining room, freshly baked sweets were already on the table—coffee was brewing in the kitchen—awaiting the end of our meeting when the much anticipated social would begin.

In some ways, the gathering was similar to hundreds of others that had been held over the previous nine decades since the group's first meeting, on April 23, 1909.

None of the ladies who would share their memories on this day were present when the club was formed. Unfortunately, most realized that they were probably the club's final group of members. And, by default, one of them would be charged with the difficult task to write the last set of minutes and close the book in the not too distant future.

Their predecessors started holding the meetings a long time ago, when most people residing in the area around Kelton never saw a horseless buggy, or used that new invention the telephone, nor heard sounds broadcast through the radio.

People at that time didn't know the term "World War," never dreamed of watching a television set or couldn't imagine riding in a aeroplane. William Howard Taft was the country's president, and the big news was that Admiral Robert E. Peary had reached the North Pole.

Life was simple, work was hard and entertainment was something you had to make for yourself. That's part of the reason the Kelton Afternoon Ladies' Club was formed.

Today, 94 years later, less than a dozen women, most of whom reside within 8 miles of the small Pennsylvania town, meet four times a year to catch up on the latest news, pass around pictures of their grandchildren, and keep alive an ever-growing number of shared memories.

Hostess Betty Hannum, 82, has been a club member for 54 years. For Jean Steele, 82, of West Grove, Pennsylvania, it's been 50 years since she attended her first meeting. Polly Barnes, 76, also of West Grove, proclaims 40 years with the ladies. Newcomers Anne McMahon, 81, of West Grove and Margaret Hickman, 72, of nearby Lincoln, Pennsylvania, both have been involved for about 20 years. Beth Hannum Thomas, 50, of Newark, Delaware, the daughter of Betty Hannum, is a birthright member, enrolled on the day she was born.

According to official records (the club has a half-dozen, worn leather volumes containing hand-written accounts of all meetings held since 1916) the group was formed to give farm women a day away from their routine chores, and their husbands. It provided a comfortable setting for them to do their fancy needlework and talk to neighboring women about shared interests and experiences.

It was started by several sisters who were members of the Nelson family, said Betty Hannum, who was president when the club celebrated its golden anniversary in 1959. She also served in that role in 1989, during the group's 80th year celebration. Betty said the farm women used to hold meetings in each other's homes, a tradition that has continued to this day.

A look at the first minutes book—with records of events from 1916 through 1929—reflects activities at gatherings and comments about significant historical events.

In 1918: "Some did not get here on account of the Spanish Influenza in their homes. Churches and schools were closed for five weeks. It is said [it has been] 100 years ago today since the churches have all been closed. At that time it was Yellow Fever. This time Spanish Influenza, or Black fever."

Later that year: "Nov. 11, the Armistice was signed. It was a sweet sound to hear the bells ringing and the whistles blowing in hopes of the longed for Peace. The word went forth 'The War is Over.'"

In 1926: "At this meeting, it was decided to let the two Mrs. Reynolds' dues for membership go toward the flower fund, as we already had started. And each member paying ten cents every year to the treasurer, Mrs. Steele, so as to have money ahead when it is needed for flowers in case of sickness and death."

In 1927: "To use a slang phrase, those with colds were 'out of luck' when it came to the amusing game our hostess had prepared. Eleven little tubes containing different liquids were passed. We were to ascertain their contents by smelling them. Number three was the greatest mystery and novelty in these prohibition days. First and second prizes

were given to the two naming the most. We were served with dainty and delicious refreshments."

In 1929, a newspaper article headline proclaimed the "Twentieth Anniversary" of the Kelton Ladies' Club and described the gathering at "The Oaks" in Oxford, Pa. Present were friends and husbands at a "banquet style" event. The lengthy article included the menu, the musical selections performed, the names of all hostesses and their guests and the decor of the room and table arrangements.

During its early days, the club met up to 14 times a year, and ice and snow storms did not cancel the winter gatherings.

Currently, the club meets quarterly, with two regular meetings and a Christmas Party and summer picnic. Up to only a few years ago, the ladies met 10 times a year, taking time off in January and February because of the strong possibility of inclement weather. Jean Steele said in the early days the meetings were held more often and the farm women met throughout the year, regardless of the weather.

Betty Hannum said the club starts each meeting by going over old business and hearing a report from the treasurer. The club members send cards to the sick and flowers to relatives of the deceased. They celebrate each other's birthdays and arrange programs, which include slide shows of trips, poetry readings, and musical entertainment performed by friends and relatives—often children. In the past, they would mark their five-year anniversary celebrations with a dinner at the Red Rose Inn in nearby Jennersville, Pennsylvania, only a mile or two up the road.

The member who serves as the monthly hostess is responsible for refreshments, and that usually means a fantastic dessert.

Members agreed that the club meetings were famous for their delicious desserts, so much so that

few participants needed to have a large meal anytime soon afterwards.

Betty Hannum said the purpose of the club has remained the same over its nine-decade history. "To break up the daily routine. And it's nice since we all know each other, some of us for a long time, for almost 50 years."

"People know each other around this area," said Jean Steele, "with the high school and the kids whose parents and grandparents went there. People don't tend to move away, but we're getting a lot more people moving in. So it's nice to get together with old friends. In this busy world, we don't take time to visit anymore. But we've all found that we seem to make time for the Kelton Ladies' Club."

Betty Hannum said the club has changed dramatically. Ladies would display their wedding and anniversary gifts at meetings, and members would come over to see new additions to each family. "But," she added, "now we haven't had births anymore."

Margaret Hickman recalled coming to meetings with her mother, so Margaret joined to carry on the family tradition and keep in touch with living remnants of her past.

Polly Barnes pointed out that she was "asked" to join. And Betty Hannum agreed that in earlier times invitations to become a member were much more formal.

Anne McMahon said she sometimes "thinks about whether we'll all be able to navigate to get here."

In one volume of the club history, historian Anna W. Russell's longhand notes in 1956 announced the beginning of a new session of meetings: "Another year has passed by, my how the time

does fly. We are entering into the forty-seventh birthday of our club and still look forward to happy times together."

In the midst of the interview session the joyous times were still evident. Some of the ladies engaged in muted conversation, exchanging memories about the young children—now grown adults with families of their own—who used to provide musical and dramatic entertainment "right over there near the fireplace."

Another duo talked about their husbands, some now deceased, who had attended the annual picnics.

With the mention of a name or an event, images seemed to flash, and words and phrases seemed to reinforce memories of a person long deceased or a friend or family member who had moved away.

All six women agreed that their periodic meetings are important, if for no other reason than to help preserve precious moments that are important links to wonderful times in their lives.

> *Unfortunately, most of the women realized that they were probably the club's final group of members. And, by default, one of them would be charged with the difficult task to write the last set of minutes and close the book in the not too distant future.*

"Stability," is what the club means to me, Jean Steele said. "It is something that has never changed."

For Polly Barnes it's "beautiful relationships."

"It's the closeness of friendships," said Anne McMahon. "If I need somebody, I could call and they would do whatever I might ask."

"I've enjoyed sharing experiences with these gals," said Betty Hannum. "I've been friends with Jean for 60 years, at least. We know each other from high school."

But one wonders, in an age of microwaves, satellite technology, computers, cell phones and the passing of the Millennium, how long the few remaining groups like the Kelton Afternoon Ladies' Club—that represent the essence of rural, middle America—will be able to survive.

Of the remaining 11 members, some have moved away and only correspond through the mail or by phone. The few who reside nearby are reaching their golden years, and the possibility of new members is not even discussed.

"I sometimes wonder about how long it will last," admitted the late Frances Miller, during a newspaper interview celebrating the club's 80th anniversary in 1989. "I think it would be nice if it lasted 100 years, we've only got 20 more to go."

"Hopefully our daughters will carry things along," said Betty Hannum, "but I know they're busy with work and children right now."

Betty's daughter, Beth Hannum Thomas, recalled how her two sons, Noah and Adam, had performed for the club on several occasions and have distributed presents to the members at the annual Christmas meeting, usually held in their grandmother's Kelton home. But now they are college students and attending the ladies club meeting would be as remote as studying math on a Friday night.

"I can really appreciate that the club is a part of my personal history," said Beth. "And I can remember my grandmother and mother hosting the Christmas meetings all of my life. I see women here who have been friends for so long. I don't think I have a friend that I have known in the same way and for as long as these women have. But I have a full-time job, and try to volunteer at my church. Often I just seem to run out of time. I'd like to make the club a priority, but that's not always possible. My mother hopes I'll carry on this family tradition. Maybe someday I can."

Author's note: One week after visiting with the Kelton Afternoon Ladies' Club, I received a handwritten thank-you card from Betty Hannum, the day's hostess. It said, in part, "Thank you so much for coming to talk with us on Saturday. The ladies really enjoyed your visit. This Saturday we are invited to lunch with a member who has moved to Lewes, Del. (Betty Sensenig lived in West Grove.) Not too many of us are going to be free to go. Do you know of any other group of such busy old ladies? Again, many thanks. My regards to your wife.
Sincerely, Betty."

That's how things are done, in proper fashion, by the Kelton Afternoon Ladies' Club.

A Beautiful Day in the Neighborhood

Photograph by Kathy F. Atkinson

One of the highlights of working on this project was being a part of the book cover photo session, held at the Delaware Agricultural Museum and Village.

On a sunny, summer, Saturday morning, 28 of the 56 folks featured in this book traveled to Dover, Delaware, and posed for several group pictures in front of a number of buildings, including a genuine, old-fashioned general store. Certainly, the large gathering created a bit more of a fuss than normally graced the building's front porch in the good old days of the early 1900s. And the laughing, conversing, yarn spinning and good natured joking on July 12, 2003, must have awakened a few of the old store's lingering ghosts.

Chuck Wehrle, a U. S. Coast Guard photographer who recorded the historic scenes at D-Day in 1944, stood beside Felix Cartagena, Newark's well-known Bubble Man. Wrestling ring announcer Billy K joked with Richard Humphreys, Lancaster

County's Gnome Man; and Billy Shutt, at 15, the youngest character in the book (who was there because his Uncle Joe Smolka took the teenager to the Grammy Awards in Madison Square Garden for his birthday), seemed a little bit stunned standing in the midst of warriors, collectors, re-enactors, treasure finders, artists and hobbyists.

The assemblage represented the wide mix of the region's fascinating, but often overlooked, people. George Reynolds and Ron Thomas, two experienced archaeologists, shared stories about their work as Jim McCloy, coauthor of *The Jersey Devil* exchanged remarks with Army Air Corp veteran Ray Russo, who was involved in 'The Last Mission' flown in World War II in August 1945.

Pennsylvania ghost hunter Rick Fisher was fascinated by craftsman Ted Stegura's lighthouse, which was created from trashed items, and Dean Rice talked about his preservation work with the Turkey Point Lighthouse, located outside North East, Maryland.

Dover Post publisher Jim Flood Sr. commented that the mix of characters was both fascinating and colorful.

Part of the color, of course, was provided by the distinctive attire some folks wore and the objects several of the others brought, all trying to visually represent their claim to their book chapter.

Lincoln license plate collector George Kreigh (he has about 6,000) wasn't surprised that he and Wilmington foul ball chaser Jay Lutz (with more than 600 in his archive) had much to share. And Delaware collectors Regina and Ken Brown of Smyrna, dressed in Colonial-era attire, were drawn immediately to Elkton's Joanna Alford, also in an early American period costume. Eventually a crowd gathered in their area, for a number of people wanted to know what is was like when Joanna discovered a letter written by Thomas Jefferson that had gone undiscovered for more than 200 years.

Elkton historian Mike Dixon discussed the documents and holdings of the agricultural museum with its executive director Linda Chatfield. Chubby Imburgia—of the Philadelphia Eagles chain gang, and wearing his black-and-white striped uniform—shared stories of his Sunday afternoons on the Veterans Stadium sidelines with ferryboat captain Jim Harris, who talked about the cruises he conducts along the Delaware River.

And there was even a reunion. Ted Stegura and Ron Thomas grew up in the same area of Pennsylvania's coal mining country and the noise from their back slapping and laughing about the "old days back home in Uniontown" attracted a bit of attention.

Part of the morning fun was playing a silent game of connect the dots with human beings, thus confirming the belief that if you live in this wonderful section of the mid-Atlantic, there's a chance you'll have something in common with someone else.

Joanna Alford knew Mike Dixon, who knew George Reynolds, who knew Ron Thomas, who knew Ted Stegura, who knew Joe Smolka.

Newark's Billy K knew Wilmington baseball re-enactor Ron Whittington, who knew author and politician Roger Martin of Middletown, who knew Dover newspaperman Jim Flood Sr.

Polka musician Joe Smolka knew Felix Cartegena, since years ago they had appeared on the same state park entertainment program.

The Gnome Man and blacksmith Joe Daddiego drove down together from Pennsylvania, and Linda Chatfield was eager to talk to Joe and show him the village's blacksmith shop. But that was after she talked to Vicki and Nancy Pearson about getting some flags for the museum from their Delaware souvenir and flag shop in Stanton.

Trying to keep order and direct the animated mob scene fell on the shoulders of my wife, the book's art director, Kathleen Okonowicz. She and photographer Kathy Flickinger Atkinson selected the setting for the cover picture and also decided upon the scenes used to begin each of the book's three sections—"Friends," "Neighbors" and "Folks Down the Road."

Coauthor Jerry Rhodes and my grandson, A. J. Marino, volunteered for the toughest job, going into the air-conditioned conference room to set out (and, no doubt, test out) the refreshments. As Kathy Photo (Flickinger Atkinson) lined up the main cast for her shots, a half-dozen personal cameras, owned by relatives and friends of the book folks, snapped along the sidelines. The amateur photographers were eager to capture their private documentation of the moment.

And as the characters and collectors, artists and authors, old warriors and lone lad moved from General Store to Sawmill, from Covered Bridge to Train Station to Farmhouse, new acquaintances became friends, wonderful stories were exchanged, and, most certainly, will be passed on—and that is one of the things that has made this project so worthwhile. It doesn't get much better than that.

—Ed Okonowicz
July 12, 2003

Photo Album

The photo shoot begins!

Smile!

Places Everyone!

A little to the left...no the right!
No...go back a little...no.... Wait!

Old friendships
were enjoyed.

𝕹ew friendships
were formed.

Fun and frolic filled the hot summer morning.

Keep your eye on the well-dressed guy with the tomahawk.

And, a good time was had by all.

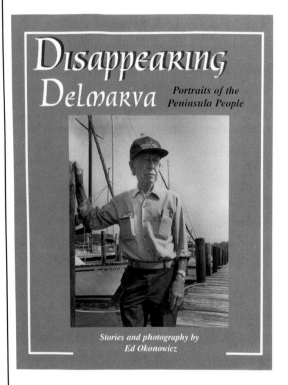

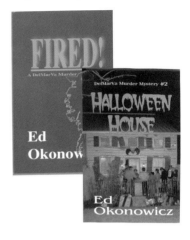
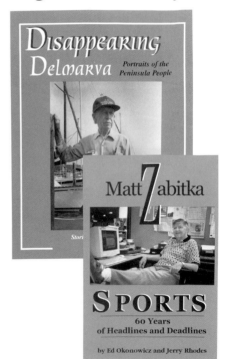

975.2   Okonowicz, Ed
OKO   Friends and Neighbors
         and Folks Down the Road

1/2006	DATE DUE		